03/09

NEB

SHOW WHAT YOU KNOW® ON THE 5TH GRADE

FCAT

FLORIDA COMPREHENSIVE ASSESSMENT TEST

D1190913

Grade 5

**TEST-PREPARATION FOR THE
FLORIDA COMPREHENSIVE
ASSESSMENT TEST**

Show What You Know
Publishing

NAME _____

Published by:

Show What You Know® Publishing
A Division of Englefield & Associates, Inc.
P.O. Box 341348
Columbus, OH 43234-1348
Phone: 1-877-PASSING (727-7464)
www.showwhatyouknowpublishing.com
www.passthefcat.com

FCAT Item Distribution information was obtained from the Florida Department of Education Web site, September 2007.

Printed in the United States of America
09 08   20 19 18 17 16 15 14 13 12 11 10 9 8 7 6 5 4 3 2

ISBN: 1-59230-292-0

Acknowledgements

Show What You Know® Publishing acknowledges the following for their efforts in making this assessment material available for Florida students, parents, and teachers.

Cindi Englefield, President/Publisher
Eloise Boehm-Sasala, Vice President/Managing Editor
Christine Filippetti, Production Editor
Jill Borish, Production Editor
Jennifer Harney, Editor/Illustrator
Charles V. Jackson, Mathematics Editor
Melissa Blevins, Assistant Editor
Angela Gorter, Assistant Editor
Trisha Barker, Assistant Editor

About the Contributors

The content of this book was written BY teachers FOR teachers and students and was designed specifically for the Florida Comprehensive Assessment Test (FCAT) for Grade 5. Contributions to the Reading, Mathematics, and Science sections of this book were also made by the educational publishing staff at Show What You Know® Publishing.

Dr. Jolie S. Brams, a clinical child and family psychologist, is the contributing author of the Test Anxiety and Test-Taking Strategies chapters of this book. Without the contributions of these people, this book would not be possible.

Table of Contents

Introduction

Dear Student:

This *Show What You Know® on the 5th Grade FCAT, Student Workbook* was created to give you practice for the Florida Comprehensive Assessment Test (FCAT) in Reading, Mathematics, and Science.

The first two chapters in this workbook—Test Anxiety and Test-Taking Strategies—were written especially for fifth-grade students. Test Anxiety offers advice on how to overcome nervous feelings you may have about tests.

The Test-Taking Strategies chapter includes helpful tips on how to answer questions correctly so you can succeed on the FCAT.

The next three chapters of this Student Workbook will help you prepare for the Reading, Mathematics, and Science FCAT.
- The Reading chapter includes a Reading Practice Tutorial, a 50-question Reading Assessment, and a Glossary of Reading Terms that will help you show what you know on the FCAT.
- The Mathematics chapter includes a Mathematics Practice Tutorial, a 55-question Mathematics Assessment, a Glossary of Mathematics Terms, and a Glossary of Mathematics Illustrations that will help you show what you know on the FCAT.
- The Science chapter includes a Science Practice Tutorial, a 55-question Science Assessment, and a Glossary of Science Terms that will help you show what you know on the FCAT.

This Student Workbook will help you become familiar with the look and feel of the FCAT and will provide you a chance to practice your test-taking skills so you can show what you know.

Good luck on the FCAT!

BLANK PAGE

Test Anxiety

Worry Less about Tests

Lots of students worry about taking tests, so if you are a test worrier, you are not alone. Many of your classmates and friends also have fearful feelings about tests, but they usually do not share their feelings. Keeping feelings to yourself is not a good idea because it just makes things worse. You may feel you are the only person with a problem and there is no one out there to help, but that is not true. Be brave. When you talk to your parents, teachers, and friends about your test-taking worries, you will feel better. You will find out that other people (even your teachers and parents) have felt worried, nervous, or scared about taking tests. You will then have other people on your team to battle the test monster.

When students feel nervous, worried, and scared, it sometimes seems there is no way out. This is also not true. Everyone can feel calm about taking tests. You don't have to be the smartest student, the most popular kid, or the fastest athlete to be a brave test taker. You just need to be willing to try; you will be amazed at how much better you will feel.

What is it Like to Have "Test Anxiety"?

One definition of the word anxiety is feeling anxious, worried, and scared. When students feel this way about taking tests, it is called test anxiety. In this chapter, the phrase test anxiety will be used a lot. Just remember that no matter what you call it, you will learn how to beat the test monster.

All sorts of students have test anxiety. It doesn't matter if a student is tall or short, shy or friendly, or a girl or a boy. Students with test anxiety might be different in a lot of ways, but they have many of the same thoughts and feelings about taking tests. Here are some of the ways students with test anxiety think and feel.

- **Students who have test anxiety don't think good things about themselves.**
  Instead of thinking about all they know, these students spend most of their time thinking about what they don't know. When their minds become filled with lists of what they don't know, there isn't any room left for remembering what they have learned and all they can do. It is like their minds are closets filled with only bad things, never good things. Imagine if you filled your closet at home with broken toys, worn-out clothes, crumpled-up papers, and all sorts of garbage. You would open up your closet and say to yourself, "Boy, my life is awful." You would ignore all the other good things you might have in your room, as well as in your life. You can bet you would not be feeling very good about yourself.

- **Students who have test anxiety "exaggerate."**
  Exaggerating means making things bigger than they are. While exaggeration makes books and movies exciting and interesting, exaggeration makes test anxiety worse. Worried thoughts grow like a mushroom out of control. "Oh no. I don't know how to do this type of math problem. See, I can't do anything. I am the worst math student ever, and I'm sure my life will be a total mess." Students with test anxiety make the worst out of situations and imagine all kinds of things that will not really happen. Their thoughts get scarier and scarier, and their futures look darker and darker. The more these students exaggerate, the more anxious and worried they become.

- **Students who have test anxiety sometimes do not feel well.**
It is important to remember that your mind and body work together. What goes on in your mind can change how your body feels, and how your body feels can change what goes on in your thinking. When your mind is filled with worries about tests, your body may also worry. You may feel your heart jumping; your stomach might hurt; your hands might become sweaty; your head may hurt; or you might even feel that you can't breathe very well. Feeling bad gets in the way of doing your best on tests. Feeling bad also makes students feel even more anxious. They say to themselves, "My heart is really beating fast, and my hands are shaking. See, I'm such a mess; I'll fail that test." Then they just become more worried and more anxious. Some students with test anxiety miss a lot of school, not because they are lazy, but because they believe they really are not feeling well. Sadly, the more school they miss, the more they fall behind, and the more nervous they feel. Their physical feelings keep them from enjoying school and facing the test monster.

- **Students who have test anxiety want to escape.**
When some students are anxious, they feel so bad that they will do anything to stay away from that feeling. They run away from problems, especially tests. Some students try to get away from tests by missing school or maybe by going to the nurse's office. This does not solve any problems because the more a student is away from the classroom, the harder the school work becomes. In the end, students who try to get away feel even worse than they did before, and they will have to take the test later on anyway. Running away from problems that cause anxiety may seem to make you feel better for a while, but it does not solve problems or make them go away.

- **Students who have test anxiety do not show what they know on tests.**
For students who are feeling worried and anxious, it's really hard to make good decisions. Instead of concentrating on the test, planning out their answers, and using what they know, students who have test anxiety blank out. They stare at the paper and see that no answer is there. They become stuck and cannot move on. Some students come up with the wrong answer because their worries get in the way of reading directions carefully or thinking about their answers. Their minds are running in a hundred different directions, and none of those directions seem to be getting them anywhere.

They forget to use what they know, and they also forget to use study skills that would help them do their best. Imagine your mind as a safe. Inside the safe are all the answers to tests and a whole lot of knowledge about school work. However, anxiety has taken away the key. Even though the answers are there, the key is gone. Your mind is racing and you can't think clearly about where you put the key. All that knowledge is trapped in there with nowhere to go. When students feel calmer about taking tests, their wonderful minds open up, and exciting ideas come pouring out.

Are You One of These "Test Anxious" Fifth Graders?

As you have seen, students with test anxiety think bad things about themselves, feel sick some of the time, and forget how to do well on tests. Do any of the kids described below remind you of yourself?

Stay-Away Stephanie

Stephanie's thoughts tell her it is better to stay away from anything that might be hard to do, especially tests. Stephanie is a good girl, but she is always in trouble for trying to avoid tests. Sometimes, Stephanie will beg her mother to allow her to stay home on test days. When that doesn't work, she will refuse to get out of bed or to catch the bus to school. You'd better believe she gets in trouble for that. Sometimes, at school, she will hide in the bathroom or go to the school nurse when test-taking time comes. Stephanie truly believes there is nothing worse than taking a test. She has so much anxiety that she forgets about all the problems that will happen when she stays away from her responsibilities. Stay-Away Stephanie feels less nervous when she stays away from tests, but she never learns to face her fears.

Worried Wendy

Wendy is the type of fifth grader who always looks for the worst thing to happen. Her mind is filled with all types of worried thoughts. She exaggerates everything bad and forgets about everything good. Her mind races a mile a minute with all sorts of thoughts and ideas about tests, all of them bad. The more she thinks, the worse she feels, and then her problems become huge. Instead of just worrying about a couple of difficult questions on a test, she finds herself thinking about failing the whole test, being made fun of by her friends, being grounded by her parents, and never going to college. She completely forgets that her parents are really nice and not strict, that her friends like her for a whole bunch of reasons, and that doing poorly on one test is not going to ruin her life. Wendy is always watching and waiting for the worst thing to happen. She spends her time worrying instead of figuring out how to do well.

Critical Chris

Chris is the type of fifth grader who spends all of his time putting himself down. No matter what happens, he always feels he has failed. While some people hold grudges against others, Chris holds grudges against himself. Even if he makes little mistakes, he can never forget them. Chris has had many good things happen in his life, and he has been successful many times. Unfortunately, Chris forgets the good and only remembers the bad. If he gets a C+ on a test, he can't remember the times he earned As and Bs. When he gets a B+ on a test, he says to himself, "I made a lot of stupid mistakes, so I didn't get an A." He never compliments himself by thinking, "I did AWESOME by getting a B+." If Chris liked himself better, he would have less test anxiety.

Victim Vince

Most fifth graders know it is important to take responsibility for themselves, but Vince wants to blame everything on others. He can't take responsibility for himself at all. He thinks everything is someone else's fault and constantly complains about friends, parents, school work, and especially about tests. He thinks his teachers are unfair and life is against him. Vince does not feel there is anything he can do to prepare for the FCAT or to help himself in any other way. Because he does not try to learn test-taking skills or understand why he is afraid, he just keeps feeling angry, sad, and worried.

Perfect Pat

Every fifth grader needs to try his or her best, but no one should try as much as Pat. Pat studies and studies, and when she is not studying, she is worrying. No matter what she does, it's never enough. She will write book reports over and over and will study for tests until she is exhausted. Trying hard is fine, but, no matter what Pat does, she feels she has not done enough. She feels worried because she cannot stop thinking that there is always more to know. Her anxiety gets higher and higher, but this does not mean she does better and better on tests. In fact, the more anxious she gets, the harder tests become. Then, when she does not do well on a test, she just wants to study more and more. What a mess! Pat should spend more time learning how to study and find time to relax.

How Can I Feel Calmer about Tests?

Test anxiety is a very powerful feeling that makes students feel they are weak and helpless. Nervous feelings can be so powerful that it sometimes seems there is nothing you can do to stop them. Worries seem to take over your mind and body and leave you feeling like you are going to lose the test-anxiety battle for sure.

The good news is that there are many things you can do to win the battle over test anxiety. If you can learn these skills in elementary school, you are on the road to success in middle school and for all the other challenges in your life.

- **Don't let yourself feel alone.**
  Although sometimes it is fun to curl up in bed and read a book by yourself, most of the time it is not very much fun to be alone. This is really true when you are feeling anxious or worried. Talking to your friends, parents, and teachers about worried feelings, especially feelings about test taking, can really help you feel better. Having test-taking worries does not mean there is something wrong with you. You might be surprised to find out that many of your friends and classmates also feel anxious about tests. You might even be more surprised to learn that your parents and teachers also had test anxiety when they were younger. They know what you are going through and are there to help you.

- **There is more than one side to any story.**
  Most fifth graders have heard a parent or teacher tell them, "There is more than one side to any story." It is easy to get in the habit of thinking about situations in a bad way instead of thinking happy thoughts. You can help yourself feel better about your life and about taking tests by training yourself to think about things from a happy point of view.

  Think about a can of soda pop. Get out a piece of paper and a pen or pencil. Now, draw a line down the middle of the paper. On one side, write the heading "All the bad things about this can of soda pop." On the other side of the paper, write the heading "All the good things about this can of soda pop." Fill in the chart with your thoughts about the can of soda pop. When you are finished, your chart might look like the one below.

All the bad things about this can of soda pop	All the good things about this can of soda pop
Not an attractive color	*Easy-to-read lettering*
It's getting warm	*Nice to have something to drink*
Not much in the can	*Inexpensive*
Has a lot of sugar	*Recyclable aluminum cans*

Look how easy it is to write down either good things or bad things about a silly can of soda pop. That can of soda pop is not good or bad; it's just a can of soda pop. You can either look at it in a good way, or you can think about everything bad that comes to your mind. Doesn't the same thing hold true for tests? Tests are not good or bad in themselves. Tests are just a way to challenge you and to see how much you know. Studying for tests can be boring and can take up a lot of free time, but you can also learn a lot when you study. Studying can make you feel great about yourself. Even if you make some mistakes on a test, you can learn from those mistakes. You can also look at your test results and compliment yourself on how much you have learned. The way you think about tests has a lot to do with how well you will be able to show what you know. Students who have good thoughts about tests are less anxious and do better. Students who always have bad thoughts and feelings about tests usually do not do as well as they should.

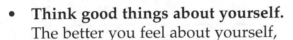

- **Think good things about yourself.**
  The better you feel about yourself,
  the better you will do on tests. This does not mean you should go around boasting and bragging to your friends about how wonderful you are. What helps most on tests is to think about all the good things you have done and learned in your past. Remind yourself of those things when you are studying for tests or even when you are taking a test.

Thinking good things about yourself takes practice. On a sheet of paper, make a chart divided into three parts like the one below. For the first part, fill in as many sentences as you can that describe "Why I Am Special." In the example below, this fifth grader has already filled in "I am very kind to animals" and "I have a good sense of humor." Next, you want to remember what you have done in your life. Make a section on the chart that reads "Things I Have Done." The fifth grader below has started his chart by remembering "I helped paint my room" and "I got a library award." Label the third column "What My Family Thinks." Don't forget to ask your family to remind you about who you are and what you have done. Make believe you are a news reporter working on a story. Interview your parents, grandparents, aunts, uncles, brothers, sisters, or anyone else who can remind you of all the good things you have done and the good person you are. Make sure to add those to your chart. This fifth grader's grandfather told him he is "smiley." Keep a chart like this in a special place where you can look at it if you are feeling anxious about tests or not very good about yourself. Reading it will make you feel better. When you feel good about yourself or when something good happens, add it to the chart. You will be amazed at what a wonderful person you are. The better you feel about yourself, the better you will be able to show what you know in school and on tests.

Why I Am Special	Things I Have Done	What My Family Thinks
I am very kind to animals.	*I helped paint my room.*	*Grandpa thinks I'm "smiley."*
I have a good sense of humor.	*I got a library award.*	

- **Everything is not a disaster.**
  If you always think a disaster is about to happen, it is called catastrophizing. A catastrophe is a disaster. It is when something terrible happens. When students catastrophize about tests, their minds go on and on thinking about terrible scenes of failure. It is like a horror movie about school, but it is worse. It is real life.

  When students stop themselves from catastrophizing, their test anxiety becomes much less noticeable. When you feel yourself catastrophizing, make yourself stop. Tell yourself, "STOP. None of this is going to happen. Tests might be hard, but they are not going to be the end of the world." Disaster thoughts have a way of getting out of hand, so the sooner you can stop yourself from thinking those thoughts, the better off you will be. Disaster thoughts get you nowhere; they only make you more anxious. The most important part is that they are not true. No matter how you do on the FCAT or on other tests in the fifth grade, your life will go on, and it will be just fine.

- **Don't make "should" statements.**
  Students make themselves anxious when they think they should do everything. They feel they should be as smart as everyone else, they should study more, and they should not feel anxious about tests. All of those thoughts are pretty ridiculous. Not everyone is going to be as smart as the next person, and you do not have to study until you drop to do well on tests. Instead of kicking yourself for not being perfect, it is better to set some reasonable goals about studying and school work. This will help you get better grades on tests and feel happier in your life.

- **Take out those bad thoughts and put in good ones.**
  If you are thinking good thoughts, it's impossible to think bad ones. People who are worried or anxious can become happier and more relaxed by thinking good thoughts. Even when something scary is happening, such as a visit to the dentist, thinking positive thoughts is very helpful. If you are thinking about something that is good or positive, it is almost impossible to think of something that is bad or negative. Keep this in mind when test anxiety starts to become a bother.

Try using some of these thoughts when you find yourself becoming worried.

Thoughts of success—"I can do it" thoughts chase away thoughts of failure. Imagining times when you were successful, such as doing well in a soccer game or figuring out a complicated brain teaser, will help you realize you can be successful. On the morning of the test, think positive thoughts. Think about arriving at school and feeling sure that you will do well on the test. Imagine closing your eyes before the test, breathing deeply, relaxing, and remembering all that you have learned. When you think about success, you will achieve success. During the test, remind yourself that you have been successful in the past and can do well in the future and on this test. This will chase away your worried thoughts.

Relaxing thoughts—You can't be worried and relaxed at the same time. Thinking about a time when you felt comfortable and happy can chase away your worries. Think about a time that you went swimming, had a pillow fight at a sleep over, or went out with your family for a huge ice-cream sundae. Soon, you will find yourself thinking about the good things in life, not the worries that trouble you.

Thoughts about beating the test monster—When you get ready to take a test, imagine you are in battle with an ugly test monster. Think about the hard work that you do to study and the good things about you. Imagine there are huge swords chasing away the test monster. Imagine the test monster running for his life as you chase away your worries and show what you know on the test. Even though it might sound silly, it works.

Copying is Prohibited © Englefield & Associates, Inc.

- **Relaxing helps chase away anxiety.**
Just as you can calm your mind, it is also important for you to relax your body. When you have test anxiety, your muscles can become stiff. In fact, your whole body might become tense. Taking deep breaths before a test and letting them out slowly as well as relaxing muscles in your body are very helpful ways to feel less anxious. You may find that not only does relaxation help you on tests, but it is also helpful for other challenging situations and for feeling healthy overall. Athletes, astronauts, and surgeons all use relaxation to help them perform their best. Here are some other methods you can try. You might also discover a different method that works well for you. Some methods will work better than others for you, so be sure to use the methods that are best for you.

Listen to music—It probably doesn't matter what type of music you listen to as long as it makes you feel good about yourself. You might want to listen to music while you study, but if it disturbs your concentration, it will not be helpful. Listening to music when you go to sleep the night before a test or in the morning while you get ready for school may also help you relax.

Develop a routine—Some people find it relaxing to have a set routine to go through each morning. Having a calm morning and a nice breakfast before you take a test such as the FCAT are always helpful. Rushing around on the morning of a test not knowing what to do next is only going to make your worries worse. When students rush and feel out of control, they begin to think, "I'll never get everything done" and, "This day is starting out terribly." Ask your family to be respectful of your routine and tell them how they can help you be more successful. This might include giving you an extra hand in getting ready the morning of the test or making sure you get to school on time.

Take care of yourself—Everyone is busy. Most fifth graders are involved in all sorts of activities, including sports, music, and helping around the house. They also love their free time and can stay out for hours skateboarding or just hanging around with their friends. Sometimes they are so busy they forget to eat breakfast or they don't get enough sleep. Eating and sleeping right are important, especially before a test like the FCAT. Even if you are not a big breakfast eater, try to find something that you like to eat, and get in the habit of eating breakfast. When you do not eat right, you feel shaky, you have a hard time thinking, and you have more anxiety. Being tired does not help either. Try to get in the habit of going to bed early enough every night so that you feel fresh and rested for the FCAT or other tests in school. Your body will be more relaxed if it is well-fed and well-rested.

Practice relaxing your body—No matter what method of relaxation you find works best for you, it is very important to practice that method so you feel comfortable with it. Practicing your relaxation method will help you during times when you are anxious, because you will know what to do to calm yourself without having to worry about it; it will become your natural response to the stressful things around you.

- **Learn to use study skills.**
  There is a chapter in this book that will help you learn test-taking strategies. The more you know about taking tests successfully, the calmer you will feel. Knowledge is power. Practice test-taking strategies to reduce your test anxiety.

- **Congratulate yourself during the test.**
  Instead of thinking, "I've only done five problems, and I have so many pages to go" or "I knew three answers, but one mixed me up," think about how well you have done so far. Tell yourself, "I've gotten some answers right, so I bet I can do more." If you concentrate on the good things you are doing during a test, you will stay calm and allow yourself to do more good things on that test.

- **Don't get down on yourself for feeling a little worried.**
  You are not alone if you feel worried about tests; everyone feels a little worried about tests. Don't be hard on yourself. If you keep telling yourself, "I'm worried, so I'll never do well," then the worst will probably happen. Instead, tell yourself, "Lots of kids get anxious. Let me just calm myself down, and I will do fine." It is important to remember that being a little worried is natural. If you know that worrying happens to everyone, it will help you defeat your anxiety and become calm and focused on the test you are taking. Remember, you are not alone in your test-taking worries.

Test-Taking Strategies

You Can Do Your Best on Tests

Most students want to do their best on tests. Tests are an important way for teachers to know how well students are doing and for students to understand how much progress they are making in school. The Florida Comprehensive Assessment Test (FCAT) helps schools find out how well students are learning. This helps teachers and principals make their schools even better. You can do the best job possible in showing what you know by learning how to be a good test taker.

It is not possible to do a good job without the right tools. Test-taking strategies are tools to help you show what you know on tests. Everyone needs good tools to fix a problem. It doesn't matter whether the problem is taking the FCAT or fixing a broken bicycle; without good tools, it's hard to be a success. Think about what would happen if your bicycle breaks and you do not have the right tools to fix it. You might know a lot about bicycles, but you can't show what you know unless you have the correct tools to fix it. You might know that the bolts on your wheels have to be put on very tightly, but how can you do that without good tools to help?

Tools are not tricks. Using good test-taking strategies is not cheating. The best students are not geniuses; they have learned to use good test-taking strategies. They learned what they need to do to show what they know when they are taking tests. You can learn these test-taking strategies, too.

Test-Taking Tools That You Can Use

Be an active learner.

You might have heard the comment, "He soaks up knowledge like a sponge." Actually, the opposite of that idea is true. Although sponges soak up a lot of water just by lying around, your brain does not work that way with information. Just because you are sitting in a classroom does not mean you are going to learn simply by being there. Students learn when they participate during the school day. This is called active learning. Active learners pay attention to what is being said. They ask themselves questions about what they hear. Active learners enjoy school, learn a lot, feel good about themselves, and usually do better on tests.

It takes time and practice to become an active learner. If you are the type of student who is easily bored or always frustrated, it is going to take some practice to use your classroom time differently. Ask yourself the following questions:

- Do I look at the teacher when he or she is talking?
- Do I pay attention to what is being said?
- Do I have any questions or ideas about what the teacher is saying?
- Do I listen to what my classmates are saying and think about their ideas?
- Do I work with others to try to solve difficult problems?
- Do I look at the clock and wonder what time school will be over, or do I enjoy what is happening during the school day and wonder how much I can learn?
- Do I think about how my school work might help me now or in the future?

The more you actively participate in school, the more you will learn and the better you will do on tests. Think about Kristen.

There was a young girl named Kristen
Who was bored and wouldn't listen.
She didn't train
To use her smart brain,
And never knew what she was missing.

Do not rely on luck.

Although sometimes it's fun to believe in luck, luck alone is not going to help you do well on the FCAT or other tests. You might know a student who feels better having a lucky coin in his or her pocket or wearing a lucky pair of shoes when taking a test. That is fine, but the best way to do well on a test is to take responsibility for yourself by taking the time and effort to do well. It is easy to say to yourself, "It's not my fault that I did poorly. It's just not my lucky day." If you believe in luck and not in your own skills, you aren't going to get very far. Students who feel they have no control over what happens to them usually receive poor grades and do not do well on tests. Don't be like Chuck.

There was a cool boy named Chuck
Who thought taking tests was just luck.
He never prepared,
He said "I'm not scared,"
When his test scores appear, he should duck.

Do your best every day!

Fifth grade is not an easy year. All of a sudden, the work seems really hard. Fifth-grade teachers are getting their students ready for middle school and are giving them more responsibility (and probably a lot more homework). Sometimes it feels like you could never learn all you need to know to do well on the FCAT. Many students begin to feel hopeless, and, sometimes, it seems easy just to give up.

Students are surprised when they find out that, if they just set small goals for themselves, they can learn an amazing amount. Do you know that if you learn just one new fact every day of the year, at the end of the year, you will know 365 new facts? Think about what happens if you learn three new facts every day. At the end of the year you will have learned 1,095 new facts. When you think about the FCAT or other tests that you have to take in school, try to think about what you can learn step by step and day by day. If you try every day, you will be surprised at how all of this learning adds up to make you one of the smartest fifth graders ever. Think about Ray.

There was a smart boy named Ray,
Who learned something new every day.
He was pretty impressed
With what his mind could possess
His excellent scores were his pay.

Get to know the FCAT.

Most fifth graders are probably pretty used to using their own CD players, televisions, and alarm clocks. They know how to use all of the controls to get the loudest sound, the clearest picture, or the early wake up. Now, imagine you are asked to use some electronic equipment that you have never seen before. You would probably think to yourself, "Where is the volume control? How do I put channels in memory? I don't even know how to change the channels to begin with. How do I put the battery in this thing?" You would probably spend a lot of time trying to figure out how everything works.

Now think about the FCAT. It will be very hard to do a good job on the FCAT if you've never seen that test before. Although the FCAT is a test, it is probably different from tests you have taken before. Getting to know the FCAT is a great test-taking tool. The more you get used to the types of questions on the FCAT and how to record your answers, the better you will do. You will also save yourself time you can use to answer the questions instead of trying to understand how they work. Think about Sue.

There was a kid named Sue
Who thought her tests looked very new.
"I never saw this before.
How'd I get a bad score?"
If she'd practiced, she'd have had more of a clue.

Read the directions and questions carefully!

Most fifth graders think directions are pretty boring. Fifth graders have already been in school for at least six years. Many of them think they have heard every direction ever invented, and it is easy for them to tune out directions. Not paying careful attention to the question that is being asked is a very bad idea. Do not tell yourself, "These directions are just like other directions I've had many times before," or "I'm not really going to take time to read these directions because I know what the question will be." The directions on the FCAT are not there to trick or to confuse you, but you cannot do well on this test if you do not read the directions and questions carefully. Read the directions and questions slowly. Repeat them to yourself. Ask yourself if what you are reading makes sense. These are powerful test-taking strategies. Think about Fred.

There was a nice boy named Fred
Who forgot almost all that he read.
The directions were easy,
But he said "I don't need these."
He should have read them instead.

Know how to fill in those answer bubbles!

By the time you are in the fifth grade, you probably have filled in answer bubbles on tests before. Remember, if you don't fill them in correctly, your answer will not be counted. Don't forget that a computer will be "reading" your answers. If you do not fill in the answer bubble dark enough or if you use a checkmark or dot instead of a circle, your smart thinking will not be counted! Look at the examples given below.

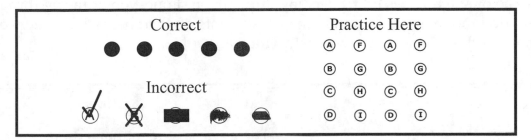

Some answers on the Mathematics section of the FCAT require the student to fill in a "response grid" that contains a numerical answer. (See page vi for examples of gridded responses.) It is very important that you take time to study and to practice filling in response grids. Answer boxes are boxes where you write your answer. Number bubbles are the places where you fill in the correct answer by clearly marking "bubbles" under the numbers that you wrote. When you are asked to use a response grid, remember the following.

- Always write your answer first in the answer boxes above the bubbles.
- Make sure you print only one digit or symbol in each answer box. Never leave a blank answer box in the middle of an answer.
- Remember those decimal points and fraction bars. Make sure to put those in if they are part of the answer.
- After you have written your numerical answer in by hand, you may then fill in the bubbles that are below each answer box. Make sure to keep everything in line. A common mistake is to fill in two answer bubbles under one number. Make sure there is only one filled-in bubble under each number or symbol. Make sure you fill in each bubble with a solid black mark that completely fills the circle. Remember, computers may be smart but they can't read your mind!

Learning how to fill in response grids takes practice, practice, and more practice! It may not be how you are used to writing mathematical answers, but it is the only way to give a right answer on the FCAT. Think about Kay!

A stubborn girl named Kay
Liked to answer questions her own way.
So her marked answer bubbles
Gave her all sorts of troubles.
Her test scores ruined her day.

Speeding through the test does not help.

The FCAT gives students enough time to read and to answer all the questions. There will always be some students who finish the FCAT more quickly than others, but this does not mean their scores will be better. It does not matter whether you finish quickly or slowly. As long as you take your time, prepare for the FCAT, pay attention to the test, and use some of the skills you have learned in this book, you should do just fine. No one will get a better score just because he or she finishes first. Speeding through a test question or racing through the whole FCAT does not help you do well. In fact, students do their best when they work carefully, not too slowly and not too quickly. Think about Liz.

There was a student named Liz
Who sped through her test like a whiz.
She thought she should race
At a very fast pace,
But it caused her to mess up her quiz.

Answer every question.

Did you know there is no penalty for guessing on the FCAT? That is really good news. That means you have a one out of four chance of getting a multiple-choice question right, even if you just close your eyes and guess. For every four questions you guess, you probably will get one (25%) of the questions right. This means it is better to guess than to leave questions blank. Guessing by itself is not going to make you a star on the FCAT, but leaving multiple-choice questions blank is not going to help you either.

It is always better to study hard and to be prepared, but everyone has to guess at some time or another. Some people do not like to guess because they are afraid of choosing the wrong answer, but there is nothing wrong with guessing if you can't figure out the correct answer. Think about Jess.

There was a smart girl named Jess
Who thought it was useless to guess.
If a question was tough,
She just gave up.
This only added to her stress.

Some students use a code to help them make good answering choices. Using your pencil in the test booklet, you can mark the following codes next to each multiple-choice question. This will help you decide what answer will be best. It will even help you to guess. Read through the codes below.

(+) Putting a "plus sign" by a choice means you think that choice is more correct than others.

(?) Putting a "question mark" by a choice means you are not sure if that is the correct answer, but it could be. You don't want to rule it out completely.

(–) Putting a "minus sign" by a choice means you are sure it is the wrong answer. If you were going to guess, you wouldn't guess that answer.

Remember, it is fine to write in your test booklet. Your pencil is a powerful tool. Use it well. Think about Dwight.

There was a smart kid named Dwight
Who marked choices that looked right.
He'd put a plus sign,
Or a dash or a line
Now the whole world knows he is bright.

Do not get stuck on one question.

One of the biggest mistakes that students make on the FCAT is to get stuck on one question. The FCAT gives you many chances to show all that you have learned. If you do not know the answer to one or two questions, your test score will not be ruined. If you spend all of your time worrying and wondering about one or two hard questions, you will not give yourself the chance to answer the questions you do know.

If you feel stuck on a question, make yourself move on. You can come back to this question later and you may be able to answer it then. This is because one question or answer may remind you of how to answer another question that seemed difficult before. Also, when you start answering questions successfully and stop being stuck, you will feel calmer and better about yourself. Then, when you go back to the hard question, you will have the confidence you need to do well. Do not tie up all of your time on one difficult question. No one knows all of the answers on the FCAT. Just circle the question that is giving you trouble and come back to it later. Think about Von.

> There was a sweet girl named Von
> Who got stuck and just couldn't go on.
> She'd sit there and stare,
> But the answer wasn't there,
> Before she knew it, all the time was gone.

Use your common sense.

You know a lot more than what you have learned in school. Most people solve problems using what they know from their daily lives as well as many things they have learned in school. When you take the FCAT, you should use everything you have learned in school, but you should also use what you have learned outside the classroom to help you answer questions correctly. This is called using common sense.

Think about a mathematics question that has to do with baking cakes. You are asked to figure out the median temperature at which cakes should be baked. You quickly figure out the answer, and your number shows 3,500° F. Does that seem right to you? If you think about what you know, you know you have never seen 3,500° F on the oven in your house. How could this answer be right? You go back and look at your answer and realize you put a decimal in the wrong place. The correct answer is 350° F. Now you have used your common sense to figure out a correct answer. Although the mathematics question might have been difficult at first, your common sense saved the day. Think about Drew.

> There was a boy named Drew
> Who forgot to use what he knew.
> He had lots of knowledge,
> He could have been in college.
> But his right answers were few.

Always recheck your work.

Everyone makes mistakes. The most mistakes are made when students feel a little worried or rushed. Checking your work is very important. Careless mistakes can easily lead to a wrong answer, even when you have figured out the answer correctly. Always read a paragraph over again if there is something you do not understand. Look to see if there is something you forgot. In the Mathematics section, look at your work to make sure you did not mix one number up with another. Check to make sure your addition, subtraction, multiplication, and division problems are all lined up neatly and are easy to read. If your numbers seem messy, you might have made a mistake. If an answer does not seem to make sense, go back and reread the question or recheck your work. Think about Cath and Jen.

A smart young lady named Cath
Always forgot to recheck her math.
She thought she was done,
But wrote eleven instead of one.
When her test score comes she won't laugh.

There was a quick girl named Jen
Who read stuff once and never again.
It would have been nice,
If she read it twice.
Her scores would be better then.

Pay attention to yourself and not to others.

What matters on the FCAT is how you do, not how your friends are doing. When you are taking a test, it is easy to look around the room and wonder how your friends are doing. This is a waste of time. Instead, use your time and energy to show what you know.

If you find your attention wandering away from the test, give yourself a little break. Think good thoughts about the FCAT and try to put scary thoughts out of your mind. Stretch your arms and feet or move around a little bit in your chair. Anything you can do to pay better attention is a great test-taking strategy. Think about Kirk.

There was a boy named Kirk
Who thought of everything but his work.
He stared in the air
And wiggled in his chair.
When his test scores come he won't look.

If you do not understand something, speak up.

No one wants to look dumb. Some students think that if they ask questions about school work or the FCAT, their classmates will think they are dumb. There is nothing wrong with asking questions. The FCAT can be a complicated test. Asking questions about the test will help you do your best. You might be surprised to learn that your classmates have the same questions that you do but are afraid to ask. Don't sit on your hands. Instead, raise them to ask important questions.

Reading

Introduction

In the Reading section of the Florida Comprehensive Assessment Test (FCAT), you will be asked questions designed to assess the knowledge you have learned so far in school. These questions are based on the reading skills you have been taught in school through the fifth grade. The questions are not meant to confuse you or to trick you but are written so you have the best opportunity to show what you know.

The *Show What You Know® on the 5th Grade FCAT, Student Workbook* includes a Reading Practice Tutorial that will help you practice your test-taking skills. Following the Reading Practice Tutorial is a full-length Reading Assessment. Both the Reading Practice Tutorial and the Reading Assessment have been created to model the 5th Grade FCAT.

About the FCAT Reading for Grade 5

Reading passages on the fifth-grade FCAT will consist of approximately 50% nonfiction (informational) and 50% fiction (literary) material. Acceptable nonfiction texts include: science and history passages, diaries, historical documents, magazine articles, essays, biographies, autobiographies, editorials, advertisements, tables, charts, and graphs. Acceptable fiction texts include: short stories, excerpts, poems, historical fiction, fables, plays, and folk tales.

Passages may include as many as 900 words and as few as 200 words. The average number of words per passage is 450. Some passages may contain words unfamiliar to fifth-grade students. These words will be clarified with a footnote.

Item Distribution and Scoring

The fifth-grade FCAT Reading uses only multiple-choice items.

You will select from four possible answer choices and fill in a bubble on the answer sheet. Although multiple-choice items sometimes ask for the recall of facts, most of the sample items demand a more complex thought process. Each multiple-choice item on the Reading Assessment is scored 0 (incorrect) or 1 (correct). Each correct answer adds one point to the total assessment score.

The following chart shows the approximate percent of raw-score points taken from each Reading Content Category.

Reading Content Categories	Points
Words and Phrases in Context	15%–20%
Main Idea, Plot, and Author's Purpose	30%–55%
Comparison & Cause/Effect	20%–45%
Reference & Research	5%–15%

Hints to Remember for Taking the FCAT Reading

Here are some hints to help you show what you know when you take the Reading Practice Tutorial and the Reading Assessment:

- Read the directions carefully. Ask your teacher to explain any directions you do not understand.

- Read the passages and questions very carefully. You may look back at a passage as often as you like.

- Answer the questions you are sure about first. If a question seems too difficult, skip it and go back to it later.

- Be sure to fill in the answer bubbles correctly. Do not make any stray marks around answer spaces.

- Think positively. Some questions may seem hard, but others will be easy.

- Check each answer to make sure it is the best answer for the question asked.

- Relax. Some people get nervous about tests. It's natural. Just do your best.

Glossary

affixes: Groups of syllables (e.g., prefixes, such as *anti-* or *post-*, and suffixes, such as *-ly* or *-ment*) which, when added to a word or a root, alter the meaning of the word.

alliteration: The repetition of the same sound, usually of a consonant, at the beginning of two or more words of a sentence or line of poetry (e.g., "Peter promptly picked the peppers").

alliterative sentences: Repeating the same initial sound in two or more words of a sentence or line of poetry (e.g., Whitman's line, "all summer in the sound of the sea").

analogy: This is a comparison of two pairs that have the same relationship. The key is to discover the relationship between the first pair, so you can choose the correct second pair (e.g., part-to-whole, opposites).

analysis: Separation of a whole into its parts for individual study.

analyze: To compare in order to rank items by importance or to provide reasons. Identify the important parts that make up the whole and determine how the parts are related to one another.

anticipation guide: A flexible strategy used to activate students' thoughts and opinions about a topic and to link their prior knowledge to new material. For example, a series of teacher-generated statements about a topic that students respond to and discuss before reading.

antonyms: Words that mean the opposite (e.g., *light* is an antonym of *dark*).

assumptions: Statements or thoughts taken to be true without proof.

author's craft: Stylistic choices the author makes regarding such components as plot, characterization, structure, scenes, and dialogue to produce a desired effect.

author's perspective: The author's subjective view as reflected in his/her written expression.

author's purpose: The reason an author writes, such as to entertain, inform, express, or persuade.

author's style: The author's attitude as reflected in the format of the author's written expression.

author's tone: The author's attitude as reflected in the word choice of the author's written expression.

automaticity: Ability to recognize a word (or series of words) in text effortlessly and rapidly.

blend: In decoding, it is the reader's act of sounding out and then combining the sounds in a word to assist in the pronunciation.

common consonant sounds: Speech sounds made by obstructing air flow causing audible friction in varying amounts. Common consonant sounds include: /b/, /d/, /f/, /g/, /h/, /j/, /k/ /l/, /m/, /n/, /p/, /kw/, /r/, /s/, /t/, /v/, /w/, /ks/, /y/, /z/.

common inflectional ending: A common suffix that changes the form or function of a word, but not its basic meaning, such as "-ed" in "sprayed," "-ing" in "gathering."

common sight words: Words that are immediately recognized as a whole and do not require word analysis for identification. These words usually have irregular spellings.

Glossary

common vowel patterns: A vowel is the open sound. The mouth must be open to produce the sound of a vowel in a syllable. The most common vowel patterns are the sound/spellings that students encounter most frequently in text (e.g., ea, ee, oi, ow, ou, oo).

comprehension monitoring strategies: Strategies used to monitor one's reading by being aware of what one does understand and what one does not understand. The reader's awareness determines which comprehension-repair strategies to apply.

comprehension-repair strategies: Strategies used by a reader to regain comprehension as a result of comprehension monitoring. These strategies include but are not limited to: rereading, word recognition strategies, looking back, reading ahead, slowing down, paraphrasing by sections, using context, and taking notes. (Also referred to as "fix-up strategies.")

comprehension strategies: A procedure or set of steps to follow in order to enhance text understanding (e.g., making inferences, predicting outcomes).

concepts of print: Insights about the ways in which print works. Basic concepts about print include: identification of a book's front and back covers and title page; directionality (knowledge that readers and writers in English move from left to right, top to bottom, front to back); spacing (distance used to separate words); recognition of letters and words; connection between spoken and written language; understanding of the function of capitalization and punctuation; sequencing and locating skills.

content/academic text: Text from literature, Science, Social Studies, Mathematics, and other academic areas that students need to read to be academically successful in school.

content/academic vocabulary: Terms from literature, Science, Social Studies, Mathematics, and other academic vocabulary that students need to know to be successful readers (e.g., "integer" in Mathematics and "pioneer" in Social Studies).

context: The social or cultural situation in which the spoken or written word occurs and is often used to refer to the material surrounding an unknown word.

context clues: Information from the surrounding text that helps identify a word or word group. These could be words, phrases, sentences, illustrations, syntax, typographic signals, definitions, examples, and restatements.

culturally relevant: Reading materials to which students in a classroom can identify or relate. Depending on the student cultural make-up in a classroom, relevant reading material can change from year to year.

decodable text: Reading materials that provide an intermediate step between words in isolation and authentic literature. Such texts are designed to give students an opportunity to learn to use their understanding of phonics in the course of reading connected text. Although decodable texts may contain sight words that have been previously taught, most words are wholly decodable on the basis of the letter-sound and spelling-sound correspondences taught and practiced in phonics lessons.

directionality: Understanding that print in English progresses from left to right and top to bottom.

electronic sources: Resources for gathering information, such as the Internet, television, radio, CD-ROM encyclopedia, and so on.

Glossary

elements of style: Word choice, voice, sentence structure, and sentence length.

environmental print: Any print found in the physical environment, such as street signs, billboards, labels, and business signs.

figurative language: Word images and figures of speech used to enrich language (e.g., simile, metaphor, personification).

fluency: Ability to read a text quickly with accuracy and expression; freedom from word-identification problems that might hinder comprehension in silent reading or the expression of ideas in oral reading; automaticity.

foreshadowing: A literary technique of giving clues about an event before it happens.

functional document: A technical document, such as a business letter, computer manual, or trade publication that assists one in getting information in order to perform a task.

generalize: Taking what is known and using it to make an inference about the nature of similar text. Generalizations lead to transferable understandings that can be supported by fact. They describe the characteristics of classes or categories of persons, places, living and nonliving things, and events.

genres: Terms used to classify literary and informational works into categories (e.g., biography, mystery, historical fiction, poetry).

gist: The most central thought or idea in a text.

graphic features: Features that illustrate information in text, such as graphs, charts, maps, diagrams, tables, etc.

graphic organizer: Organizers that provide a visual representation of facts and concepts from a text and their relationships within an organized frame. Valuable instructional tools used to show the order and completeness of a student's thought process graphically.

icons: Symbols on a computer screen that represent a certain function, command, or program on the computer's hard drive. When an icon is clicked on, some action is performed, such as opening or moving a file or making computing more user-friendly.

idiom: A word used in a special way that may be different from the literal meaning (e.g., "you drive me crazy" or "hit the deck").

independent level: The level at which the student reads fluently with excellent comprehension. The accuracy with which the student reads is 95–100%.

infer: To understand something not directly stated in the text by using past experience and knowledge combined with the text.

inference: The reasoning involved in drawing a conclusion or making a logical judgment on the basis of indirect evidence and prior conclusions rather than direct evidence from the text.

inferred: To reach a specific conclusion. (Using past experiences and knowledge combined with text evidence.)

inflectional endings: A letter or group of letters, which when added to the end of a word, does not change its part of speech, but adjusts the word to fit the meaning of the sentence (e.g., girl, girls; jump, jumped; big, bigger).

Copying is Prohibited   © Englefield & Associates, Inc.

Glossary

informational/expository text: A form of written composition that has as its primary purpose explanation or the communication of details, facts, and discipline- or content-specific information (e.g., content area textbooks, encyclopedias, biographies).

instructional level: The level at which the student can make maximum progress in reading with teacher guidance. The accuracy with which the student reads is 90–94%.

irony: The use of words to convey the opposite of their literal meaning: the words say one thing, but mean another.

keyword searches: A key term or phrase the computer uses in order to begin an online search for specific information.

language registry: The systematic differences of language use determined by regional, social, or situational changes (e.g., a child might say "yup" at home but would be expected to say "yes" at school).

letter patterns: Common letter groupings that represent specific sounds (e.g., "ing" in "string").

literary devices: Techniques used to convey or enhance an author's message or voice (e.g., idiom, figurative language, metaphor, exaggeration, dialogue, and imagery).

literary/narrative genres: Categories used to classify literary works, usually by form, technique, or content (e.g., novel, essay, short story, comedy, epic).

literary/narrative text: Text that describes action or events; usually includes a problem (conflict), solution, and resolution; usually but not always, fiction.

main idea: The gist of a passage; central thought; the chief topic of a passage expressed or implied in a word or phrase; the topic sentence of a paragraph; a statement in sentence form which gives the stated or implied major topic of a passage and the specific way in which the passage is limited in content or reference.

mental imagery: Words or phrases that appeal to one or more of the five senses allowing the reader to form mental pictures or images while reading.

metaphor: A figure of speech that compares two things without using the words *like* or *as* (e.g., laughter is the best medicine).

mood: The emotional state of mind expressed by an author or artist in his/her work, or the emotional atmosphere produced by an artistic work.

multiple meaning words: Words with the same spelling and/or pronunciation which have more than one meaning depending on their context, such as, "The wind blew" and "Please wind the clock."

non-technical documents: In this context, non-technical refers to documents (e.g., memos, lists, job applications) in which the content and vocabulary are not tied to a specific subject.

oddity tasks: In phonemic awareness, identifying which word in a set of three or four that has the "odd" sound (e.g., run, rug, and toy).

onomatopoeia: Words whose pronunciations suggest their meaning; words that describe and represent a sound (e.g., meow, buzz).

Glossary

onset and rime: Parts of spoken language that are syllables. An onset is the initial consonant (s) sound of a syllable (the onset of bag is *b-*; of swim, is *sw-*). A rime is the part of the syllable that contains the vowel and all that follows it (the rime of bag is *-ag*; of swim, *-im*). Not all syllables or words have an onset, but they all have a rime (e.g., the word or syllable "out" is a rime without an onset).

oral language structure: Spoken language has five linguistic systems. They include the phonological (sounds of language), the syntactic (order and grammar), the semantic (meanings), the pragmatic (social interactive), and lexicon (vocabulary).

organizational features: Tools the author uses to organize ideas (e.g., caption and headings).

personification: A figure of speech in which nonhuman objects, such as ideas, objects, or animals, are given human characteristics (e.g., "flowers danced about the lawn").

persuasive devices: A technique the author uses to move the reader to his/her point of view such as bias, overgeneralization, and association.

phoneme: The smallest unit of sound in a spoken word that makes a difference in the word's meaning.

phonemic awareness: The ability to hear, identify, and manipulate individual sounds (phonemes) in spoken words.

phonics: The understanding that there is a predictable relationship between phonemes (the sounds of spoken language) and graphemes (the letters and spellings that represent those sounds in written language).

phonological awareness: A general understanding of the sound structure of words, including rhymes, syllables, and phonemes.

plot: The structure of the events in a story usually including conflict, rising action, climax, solution, and resolution.

point of view: The perspective from which a narrator tells the story. The three points of view are first person, third person, and omniscient.

predict: To foresee what might happen in a text based on a reader's background knowledge or schema.

predictions: Foretelling what might happen next in a story or poem by using a reader's background knowledge or schema.

prefix: An affix attached before a base word or root, such as *re-* in reprint.

primary sources: The original source of resource information (e.g., newspaper, letter, encyclopedia, book).

print conventions: The rules that govern the customary use of print in reading and writing including directionality of print, punctuation, and capitalization.

prior knowledge: The knowledge that stems from previous experience. Note: Prior knowledge is a key component of the schema theory of reading comprehension.

propaganda techniques: Methods used in creating propaganda, such as bandwagon, peer pressure, repetition, and testimonials or endorsements.

Glossary

pull-down menus: A computer term that refers to a list of words that appears when the cursor is on a menu item. Also called a drop-down list box.

questioning strategies: In these strategies a reader may ask questions about a text before, during, and after reading and then searches for answers [e.g., Question Answer Response (QAR); Survey, Question, Read, Recite, Review (SQ3R)].

root words: Meaningful base form of a complex word, after all affixes are removed. A root may be independent, or free, as "read" in unreadable, or may be dependent, or bound, as "liter" (from the Greek word for letter) in illiterate.

sarcasm: A remark used to "make fun of" or "put down" someone or something. The remark is not sincere and is actually intended to hurt someone's feelings. The tone of the speaker and the context of the situation are clues to the use of sarcasm.

scan: To examine or read something quickly, but selectively, for a purpose.

schema: The accumulated knowledge drawn from life experiences that a person has to help understand concepts, roles, emotions, and events.

secondary sources: Sources of information that are derived from primary or original sources.

segment: The act of separating the sounds in a word in order to assist decoding or spelling.

semantic mapping: A graphic display of a cluster of words that are meaningfully related.

sentence structure: Any of a number of basic sentence types in a language. The pattern or structure of word order in sentences, clauses, or phrases.

sequence: The arrangement or ordering of information, content, or ideas (e.g., chronological, easy to difficult, part to whole).

sequential: Marked by an arrangement or order of information, content, or ideas, such as part to whole, easy to difficult, etc.

setting: The time(s) and place(s) in which a narrative takes place.

short vowel sounds: The sound of /a/ as in cat, /e/ as in hen, /i/ as in fit, /o/ as in hot, /u/ as in pup.

sight words: Words that are immediately recognized as wholes and do not require word analysis for identification.

similes: Figures of speech comparing two unlike things usually using *like* or *as* (e.g., Like ancient trees, we die from the top).

skim: To read or glance through quickly.

story elements: The critical parts of a story including character, setting, plot, problem (conflict), and solution. At upper grades, the term problem changes to conflict.

story structure: The pattern of organization in narration that characterizes a particular type of story.

structural analysis: The identification of word-meaning elements, such as *re-* and *read* in reread, to help understand the meaning of a word as a whole.

Glossary

sub-genres: Genres within other genres (e.g., haiku is a sub-genre of poetry, and mystery is a sub-genre of fiction).

subplot: A minor collection of events in a novel or drama that have some connection with the main plot and should, (1) comment on, (2) complicate/defeat, or (3) support the main plot.

suffix: An affix attached to the end of a base, root, or stem that changes meaning or grammatical function of the word (e.g., -*en* added to *ox* to form *oxen*).

summarize: To determine what is important in the text, condense this information, and put it into the students' own words.

summary: A synthesis of the important ideas in a text presented in a condensed form.

syllabification: Division of words into syllables. A syllable is a word part that contains a vowel, or in spoken language a vowel sound (e-vent; news-pa-per; ver-y).

synonyms: A word having a similar meaning to the meaning of another word (e.g., *sketch* is a synonym of *draw*).

task-oriented text: Text written specifically to direct the reader as to how to complete a task.

technical: Content or vocabulary directly related to specific knowledge or information in a career or interest area.

text complexity: Text demands on the reader increase substantially throughout the grades. Items that influence complexity of text include: highly specialized vocabulary and concepts; abstract concepts presented with minimal context; increased concept load/density; readability considerations; and unique writing patterns in informational text.

text features: A prominent characteristic of a particular type of text, such as chapter titles, subheadings, and boldface words in a history text.

text organizational structures: Text is structured in certain ways. The five text structures that students are most likely to encounter are cause-effect, compare/contrast, description, problem/solution, and chronological or time order.

theme: A topic; a major idea or proposition broad enough to cover the entire scope of a literary work. Note: A theme may be stated or implicit, but clues to it may be found in the ideas that are given special prominence or tend to recur in a work. Theme often refers to a lesson the characters or readers are meant to learn.

unfamiliar text: Unseen, unpracticed reading material.

vocabulary strategies: A systematic plan to increase understanding of words (e.g., categorizing and classifying, semantic mapping, semantic feature analysis, concept of definition maps, analogies, using the dictionary and other reference materials, using word parts, using morphemic analysis, using context clues).

word families: A collection of words that share common orthographic rimes (e.g., thank, prank, dank).

word recognition strategies: Strategies for determining the pronunciation and meaning of words in print.

Reading Practice Tutorial

Directions for Taking the Reading Practice Tutorial

The Reading Practice Tutorial contains eight reading passages, 20 practice questions, and an Answer Sheet. It should take about 30 to 45 minutes to read the passages and answer all the questions. You will mark your answers on the Answer Sheet on page 56 of this workbook. If you don't understand a question, just ask your teacher to explain it to you.

This section will review the Strands, Standards, and Benchmarks used to assess student achievement in the state of Florida. Following the description of each Benchmark, a sample reading passage and practice items are given. Each item gives you an idea of how the Benchmark may be assessed. Review these items to increase your familiarity with FCAT-style multiple-choice questions. Once you have read through this Practice Tutorial section, you will be ready to complete the Reading Assessment.

Sample Multiple-Choice Item

To help you understand how to answer the test questions, look at the sample test question and Answer Sheet below. It is included to show you what a multiple-choice question in the test is like and how to mark your answer on your Answer Sheet.

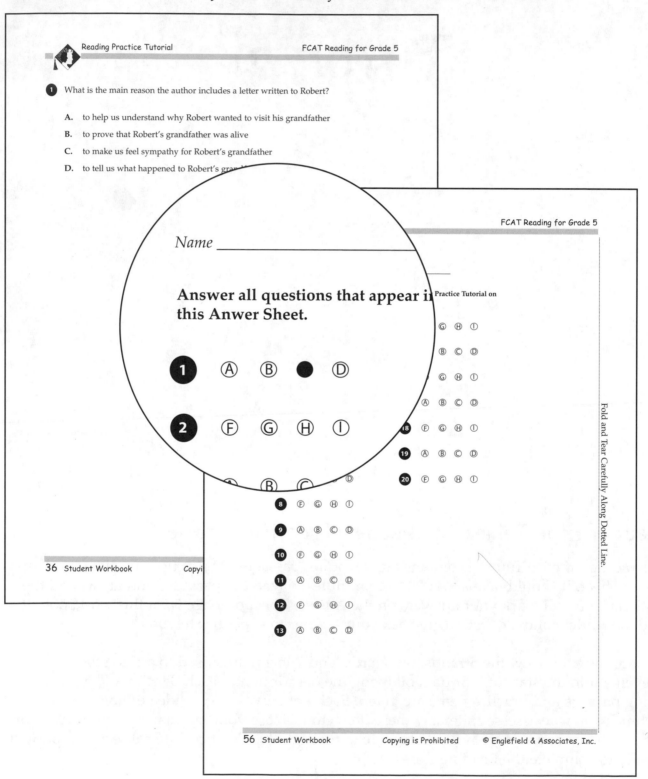

Reading Practice Tutorial

FCAT Reading for Grade 5

1 What is the main reason the author includes a letter written to Robert?

A. to help us understand why Robert wanted to visit his grandfather

B. to prove that Robert's grandfather was alive

C. to make us feel sympathy for Robert's grandfather

D. to tell us what happened to Robert's gran

FCAT Reading for Grade 5

Name _____

Answer all questions that appear in Practice Tutorial on this Anwer Sheet.

1 Ⓐ Ⓑ ● Ⓓ

2 Ⓕ Ⓖ Ⓗ Ⓘ

36 Student Workbook

56 Student Workbook   Copying is Prohibited   © Englefield & Associates, Inc.

Reading Practice Tutorial

Read the article "Hummingbirds" before answering Numbers 1 and 2.

Hummingbirds

Have you ever heard the humming sound of the hummingbird? These tiny birds get their name from the sound they make when their wings beat rapidly in the air. Your chances of catching a long gaze of one are slim to none, however. Hummingbirds don't hang around in one spot for very long.

Hummingbirds feed on the sweet nectar found within the brightly colored flowers you might find around your garden or in the backyard. They are especially attracted to bright red- and orange-colored blooms. To get to the nectar, hummingbirds extend their long tongues down into the flowers. Nectar isn't the only thing that the hummingbird likes to eat. It will also munch on tiny insects that hide out in the flowers.

One unusual characteristic about the hummingbird is its ability to fly backwards. This comes in handy when the bird flies back and forth away from flowers as it gathers nectar. It is the only bird with this unique flying ability.

Although there are about two dozen species of hummingbirds in the United States, the ruby-throated hummingbird is the most common. It can be found throughout the South. It is approximately four inches in length and is easily recognized. Male ruby throats are shiny green in color with brilliant red throats and white breasts. The female is less brightly colored and does not have a ruby throat.

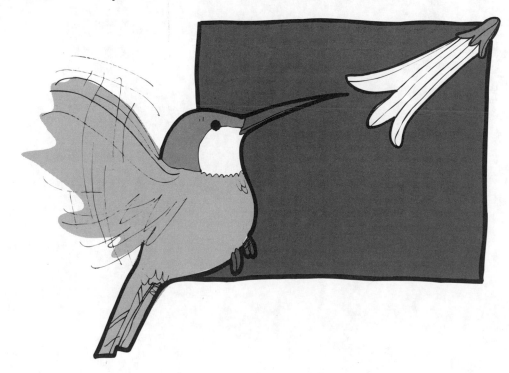

Now answer Numbers 1 and 2 on your Reading Practice Tutorial Answer Sheet on page 56. Base your answers on the article "Hummingbirds."

1 Read this sentence from the article.

> **Your chances of catching a long gaze of one are slim to none, however.**

What does the word *gaze* mean?

A. look

B. sound

C. movement

D. flight

2 Read this sentence from the article.

> **Male ruby throats are shiny green in color with brilliant red throats and white breasts.**

As used in this sentence, what does the word *brilliant* mean?

F. ignorant

G. smart

H. dazzling

I. dull

Read the story "Tucker the Squirrel" before answering Numbers 3 through 5.

Tucker the Squirrel

The afternoon sky turned a deep blue. The wind began to blow and broke off the smallest limbs of the oak trees in Jonathan's backyard. Even though it was late May, Jonathan heard on the radio that a spell of cool weather was on its way. The days hadn't become too hot yet, but he thought the crisp, fresh air felt nice just the same.

At the dinner table, Jonathan and his family talked about the change in weather and discussed plans for an upcoming trip to the lake. He picked at his green peas and daydreamed about summer, friends, and no school. After finishing dinner, Jonathan and his little sister cleaned up the kitchen and put away the dishes.

Out the window, Jonathan could see Rudy, his dog, playing with a rubber ball. Suddenly, Rudy began to bark. He barked and barked until finally Jonathan went outside to find out what all the noise was about. When he opened the door, the wind caught it and threw it into the house with a loud SMACK! He fought the gusts and slowly pulled the door closed and made his way down the porch steps. He saw Rudy nudging a small animal with his nose.

Jonathan made his way across the green grass. His hair was swirling all around his head. Carefully, Jonathan walked toward Rudy and the tiny creature. At first, he thought it was a mouse, but after a closer look, Jonathan saw that it was a baby squirrel. He looked up at the tall tree. Squirrels must have nested somewhere up there, he thought. He ran inside and called for his parents to come into the back yard.

Jonathan's dad lifted the baby squirrel into his hands to see if it was still alive. It had taken a long fall out of its nest, but it seemed to be OK. Jonathan and his dad recognized it was an Eastern Gray squirrel, just like the ones they had seen before in the park. Its eyes were still closed, and after a little research, they guessed it was only about four weeks old.

They took the squirrel inside and tried to warm it up. Jonathan's mom called the wildlife department for instructions on how to help the abandoned baby. Jonathan thought it would be a great idea to raise the baby squirrel and immediately gave it the name "Tucker." He found a large shoebox and put an old shirt inside. Then he put a heating pad underneath the box to help keep Tucker warm.

Even though Jonathan wanted to keep the squirrel as a pet, he knew that it must be released back into the wild. As soon as Tucker was old enough to find food and could survive on his own, he would be returned to the back yard where Jonathan knew he really belonged.

Now answer Numbers 3 through 5 on your Reading Practice Tutorial Answer Sheet on page 56. Base your answers on the story "Tucker the Squirrel."

3 What is the MAIN problem in the story?

    A.   Jonathan has to clean the dishes after dinner.

    B.   Jonathan's younger sister won't do her chores.

    C.   A baby squirrel has fallen from a tree.

    D.   The temperature outside is getting cold.

4 Which event happened FIRST?

    F.   Rudy, the dog, barked.

    G.   Jonathan's dad picked up the baby squirrel.

    H.   The baby squirrel fell out of its nest.

    I.   The wind began to blow.

5 Jonathan goes outside after dinner because

    A.   he wants to play baseball.

    B.   he sees the baby squirrel on the ground.

    C.   he hears his dog barking.

    D.   he doesn't want to do the dishes.

Read the article "School Uniforms" before answering Numbers 6 and 7.

School uniforms

by Amber Gianetti, Lakewood Elementary School

Last year, the school board decided Lakewood Elementary students should wear uniforms. Many parents think this is best for kids. We have to wear uniforms to school every day because somebody's mom thinks it's better for us. But in reality, school uniforms are really bad for our mental health.

Our uniforms are boring. We wear polo shirts or button-down shirts, and they have to be light blue or white. The boys wear khaki pants and brown shoes. The girls wear brown shoes and a khaki skirt. Everyday, we get up and put on the same old boring clothes.

I've talked with many of my friends. They all said putting on the same outfit every day is really depressing. We don't want to go to school depressed. It's hard to get our work done. All creativity is drained.

Our hallways are filled with students who all look the same. According to my teacher, the uniforms remind us we are all equal. While I don't disagree we are all equal, I think people send this message, not clothes. The uniforms cover up each student's uniqueness. Even though we are all equal, we are all distinct. There are differences in our school, and I think we should be allowed to wear clothes we have picked out in order to express our

unique qualities. Haven't we always been told it doesn't matter what's on the outside; it's what's inside that counts?

If teachers think uniforms are such a great idea, why don't they wear them? Lakewood teachers wear whatever they want. They are allowed to express themselves with an individual sense of style.

If the teachers had to wear the same outfit each day, I know they would feel differently about the uniform rule. Uniforms are bad for our mental health. The uniforms tell us we have to look the same to be equal, and we shouldn't express who we are. Kids shouldn't have to wear uniforms to school. We should be allowed to make our own decisions about what to wear every day.

Go On

Now answer Numbers 6 and 7 on your Reading Practice Tutorial Answer Sheet on page 56. Base your answers on the article "School Uniforms."

6 Why did the author write this article?

    F. to convince readers that students should not wear uniforms

    G. to give information on why students should wear uniforms

    H. to tell why she believes the school uniform colors should be changed

    I. to inform readers about her school's uniform rule

7 The author would MOST likely agree with which statement?

    A. Teachers at Lakewood Elementary like to wear uniforms.

    B. Uniforms encourage students to express themselves.

    C. Students cannot express themselves if they all dress the same.

    D. Uniforms help students recognize that all people are equal.

Read the articles "Alligators" and "Crocodiles" before answering Numbers 8 through 10.

Alligators are amazing animals. The American alligator lives in the southeast part of the United States where it stays warm. Most grow to be approximately[1] 10 feet long. Some of the world's biggest alligators have even grown to be 22 feet long!

Alligators have broad snouts that are flat and round. An alligator also has a tail, four short legs, skin that is tough and gray, and more than 70 sharp teeth. When the mouth is closed, you cannot see the bottom row of teeth. If a tooth falls out, another grows in to take its place. An alligator can live up to 75 years, and in its lifetime, it may change teeth over 40 times! Alligators crawl around on land and swish their tails back and forth to move through the water. They cannot control the temperature of their bodies, so if it gets too cold, they lie in the sun; if it's too hot, they float in the water.

Alligators are very sneaky hunters. They will stay in the water and wait for a fish, a frog, or a turtle to come too close and then, SNAP! They will even creep up on animals that have stopped for a quick drink, like birds or raccoons.

Like other reptiles, alligators lay their eggs on land. The mother scoops out a hole and lays as many as 50 eggs in it. She then covers the area with mud and plants and stays near the nest. About two months later, when she hears some grunting sounds, she tears the top off the nest and there are her baby alligators blinking up at her.

---

[1] **approximately:** about

CROCODILE

Crocodiles live in the tropical and subtropical regions of the world. The American crocodile can be found mostly in Florida. Like all reptiles, crocodiles are cold-blooded. This means the body's temperature depends on the environment. To stay warm, a crocodile lies in the sun. To stay cool, a crocodile lies in the shade.

The crocodile has a narrow snout. When the mouth is closed, the teeth of the lower jaw are visible. The average crocodile has about 30–40 teeth in its lower jar and has roughly the same number in its upper jaw. The jaws of the crocodiles are very powerful and are extremely important for catching food.

These reptiles eat fish, frogs, and other small aquatic animals. Some larger crocodiles have been known to feast on deer and oxen. When searching for food, crocodiles submerge themselves in water. The eyes and nose are just above the surface as the reptile waits for a chance to catch its prey.

Although it spends much of its time in the water, the female crocodile lays her eggs in sand or mud. The heat of the sun helps the eggs to hatch. Similar to the female alligator, the female crocodile will protect her nest against predators looking to make a meal of her eggs.

Copying is Prohibited   © Englefield & Associates, Inc.

Now answer Numbers 8 through 10 on your Reading Practice Tutorial Answer Sheet on page 56. Base your answers on the articles "Alligators" and "Crocodiles."

8 How are crocodiles and alligators ALIKE?

    F. The females do not protect their eggs.

    G. They are both reptiles.

    H. They both have broad snouts.

    I. You can see the bottom row of teeth when the mouth is closed.

9 Read this sentence from the article "Crocodiles."

> **Similar to the female alligator, the female crocodile will protect her nest against predators looking to make a meal of her eggs.**

Which statement is correct?

    A. A female alligator will protect a crocodile's eggs.

    B. Female alligators and female crocodiles both protect their own eggs.

    C. A female crocodile will protect an alligator's eggs.

    D. Female alligators and female crocodiles both abandon their own eggs.

10 How could someone tell the DIFFERENCE between an alligator and a crocodile?

    F. by looking at the mouths and the snouts

    G. by looking at the tails

    H. by weighing the animals

    I. by looking at the feet and the legs

Read the announcement "Kids! Don't Miss This!" before answering Numbers 11 through 13.

KIDS! DON'T MISS THIS!

Human beings aren't the only ones who build homes. All kinds of animals and insects create their own special dwellings. Whether you realize it or not, our world is covered with many different types of homes in many different places. The variety is fascinating! That's why you don't want to miss the "Homebodies" exhibit.

Sponsored by the Science Club, this event will be held Saturday and Sunday, from 1:00 p.m. until 5:00 p.m. each day. You will find all the wonderful exhibits in the Brova Elementary School gym.

The Science Club has worked long and hard, and we know you're going to be impressed! This event is going to be fun, fun, fun!

YOU WILL LEARN HOW TO MAKE YOUR VERY OWN:

- Spider webs
- Bird nests
- Beehives
- Ant farms
- Teepees
- Igloos
- Sod houses
- Log cabins
- Tents

YOU WILL SEE PICTURES FROM INSIDE:

- Bear caves
- Lion dens
- Bat caves
- English castles
- Tree houses
- And much, much more!

**This is a great family event,
and you won't want to miss a minute of it!**

ADMISSION IS FREE,
so bring your parents, sisters, brothers, neighbors, and friends.

Now answer Numbers 11 through 13 on your Reading Practice Tutorial Answer Sheet on page 56. Base your answers on the announcement "Kids! Don't Miss This!"

11 How long is this event?

    A. ⌐ four hours

    B. all weekend

    C. one day

    D. eight hours

12 What is the purpose of this announcement?

    F. to encourage people to donate supplies for building homes

    G. to invite people to a special exhibit

    H. to inform people about the duties of the Science Club

    I. to invite people to join the Homebodies Club

13 Someone who attends the exhibit will MOST likely

    A. save money in order to pay for admission.

    B. bring materials to build a birdhouse.

    C. learn about the many types of homes that are displayed.

    D. want to become a member of the Science Club.

Read the story "The Stowaway" before answering Numbers 14 through 16.

The Stowaway

Polly was no ordinary penguin. As a matter of fact, she was always getting into trouble because of her sense of adventure and her overactive imagination. She and her family lived on an iceberg just north of Antarctica.

Every day, Polly would watch the fishing boats come and go with their nets full of fresh fish to take back to the marketplace. She loved the smell of the salty air and the sound of the fishermen talking as they did their work.

She knew their routine well. They moved the boats in before sunrise and then threw out the large nets until they sank into the water. After that, the fishermen rested for awhile until the nets were full of fish and other sea creatures.

At the sound of the captain, the crew hoisted the nets up from the ocean and onto the deck of the fishing boat. The nets were released and hundreds of shiny, slippery fish fell like raindrops from the sky. Polly had watched the fisherman many times and had wondered what it must be like on the boat with all those wonderful fish.

Sometimes the fishermen would throw Polly a fish or two when the captain wasn't looking. This time her curiosity was more than she could stand. Polly dove into the icy water and swam around to the other side of the boat. She found a rope ladder that had been thrown over the side and made her way out of the water onto the boat.

She waddled as quietly as she could all around the boat hoping not to be caught by the fishermen. It was better than she imagined. She saw all kinds of gadgets and wheels and more fishing nets. She also found ropes and floating rings. Polly decided that she had seen enough, and just as she was about to dive back into the water, the captain saw her.

He chased Polly around the deck and almost caught her by the foot. Just as he was about to grab her, the captain slipped on a slimy piece of seaweed. Polly made her escape. She swam back to her home on the iceberg safely, but it wasn't the last time Polly's curiosity almost got her into trouble.

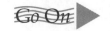

Now answer Numbers 14 through 16 on your Reading Practice Tutorial Answer Sheet on page 56. Base your answers on the story "The Stowaway."

14 What danger does Polly face in the story?

F. Polly is chased by the captain of the fishing boat.

G. Polly slips off the iceberg and can't get back up.

H. Polly is hungry.

I. Polly gets caught in the fishing boat's nets.

15 Why does Polly go aboard the fishing boat?

A. She is hungry.

B. She is curious about what is on the boat.

C. The captain invited her to come aboard.

D. She wants to free all the captured fish.

16 Read this sentence from the story.

She swam back to her home on the iceberg safely, but it wasn't the last time Polly's curiosity almost got her into trouble.

After reading this sentence, what can you predict?

F. Polly will never let her curiosity get the best of her again.

G. Polly will stay out of trouble.

H. Polly will never go aboard a fishing boat again.

I. Polly will find herself in trouble because of her curiosity.

Read the story "The Gift" before answering Number 17.

The Gift

Ming looked at the stacks of books. As she walked up and down each aisle, she quickly became confused. The dark wood shelves seemed to grow taller with each step. The books all looked the same. Each row led to another row, which led to more stacks that contained even more brightly colored books. "What have I gotten myself into?" she thought to herself. Time ticked by, and just when it seemed as though Ming would never find another human being in the maze of books, she stumbled upon a sales clerk.

The clerk's bright yellow T-shirt read, "Let Me Help You." Ming couldn't have been more pleased. "Just in time," she thought to herself. "I was about to give up on this place." Mother's Day was just around the corner, and Ming was on the hunt for the perfect gift. There was just one problem: Ming had no idea what type of book she wanted to buy.

Ming and the clerk chatted for a moment or two. Then, the lady in the yellow shirt had an idea. "When you were a little girl, did your mom like to read you stories?" Ming nodded. "You should pick out your favorite storybook. It will remind the two of you of your special memories. I'll help you write a special thank-you note on the inside cover. Your mom will love it!" The clerk spoke so quickly, Ming didn't have time to object.

The clerk was very enthusiastic as she marched Ming toward the children's book corner. Ming wasn't too sure about the idea, but her time at the bookstore had been unproductive so far. At least she was closer to finding something. After trotting through a few more rows of the dark stacks, Ming was happy to reach the children's area. The white stacks were the perfect height. Ming could even reach the top rows. The book titles were familiar, and the carpet beneath her feet featured white clouds in a blue sky.

The clerk sat patiently in a rocking chair, and Ming looked over the shelves. Some of the books she had seen before; others seemed brand new. Ming carefully studied the titles, but it wasn't until she reached the very bottom row that she found a copy of *The Magic of Myra Brown.* "This is it," she thought. The cover featured a freckle-faced redhead who wore a crooked witch's hat. A small black cat peered around Myra's leg, and the title stood out in bold red letters. "I'll take this one," she said to the clerk.

Ming pulled a wad of crumpled money from her jacket pocket. The clerk rang up the book, then found a special pen for Ming's inscription[1]. Ming thought for a moment before writing, "Mom: Thank you for always making me feel as magical as Myra. Love, Ming."

"Perfect," said the clerk.

"Thank you so much," Ming replied. She held the book tightly as she made her way out the door. Ming was proud of the special gift. She couldn't wait for Mother's Day to arrive.

[1]**inscription:** message

Now answer Number 17 on your Reading Practice Tutorial Answer Sheet on page 56. Base your answer on the story "The Gift."

17 When the clerk first gives Ming the idea of buying a children's book, how does Ming feel?

    A.   Ming knows a children's book is the perfect gift.

    B.   Ming doesn't like children's books.

    C.   Ming doesn't know if a children's book will make a good gift.

    D.   Ming's mother never read children's books.

Go On

Read the story "Funds for Food" before answering Numbers 18 through 20.

Funds for Food

Jeanette reached into the dog cage and pulled out the newspaper. It was dirty and wet and she made a face as the smell hit her nose. She loved working with the animals at the shelter, but sometimes the odors were a little overwhelming.

"Hey! Do you know where the rest of the cat food is?" asked Jessica, her twin sister, as she walked into the room. "I can only find one bag." The sisters were the best of friends and often did things together. Their favorite thing to do was volunteer at the shelter with their mother. They went off in search of more pet food, but instead of finding it, they found Mrs. Kline, the lady in charge of the shelter. She looked very unhappy.

"If you're looking for more food, there isn't any," she said. "We just don't have the money for it. Winter is just around the corner, and we've had so many new animals coming in; it's hard to keep up! I'm just not sure what we're going to do," she sighed.

Jeanette and Jessica found their mother in the laundry, washing the animal's towels and blankets. They told her the sad news.

"Do you think that there is something we could do to help, Mom?" asked Jeanette. "Could we raise some money?" Mrs. Snowden smiled; she knew when her girls got an idea to do something, they usually did it!

"Let's go talk with Mrs. Kline."

For the next two hours, the volunteers sat at the snack table and threw out all kinds of ideas for what could be done to help the shelter. Everything was discussed and, in the end, they made plans for several fund-raisers, including a bake sale, a car wash, and a yard sale. Mrs. Kline made a few phone calls and arranged for the local radio and television stations to run some ads for the fund-raisers.

The rest of the day was spent creating jars with pictures of the different pets glued onto them. Mrs. Snowden took the jars to area stores and asked the storeowners to place the jars near the checkout counter. She hoped people would donate their extra change to the shelter. Another volunteer made posters. He hung them at local pet stores. The posters asked for donations of old blankets, towels, and play toys. This would help the shelter cut costs.

Jessica and Jeanette made their own plans. For the next month, they raised money every way they could. They had a yard sale and sold toys they no longer played with. They raked the autumn leaves for their neighbors and helped their grandma clean her house and make jam. They walked Mrs. Cotton's dogs each day, and they helped with the car wash. The girls kept their earnings in a jar labeled "Funds for Food."

At the end of the month, Mrs. Snowden took the girls and the funds to the grocery store. They loaded up the car with bags of pet food. Everyone had big smiles on their faces as they walked into the shelter. Mrs. Kline was pleased to hear about all the hard work the girls had done, and she had good news for them, too.

"I talked to members of the City Council. They were so impressed at how hard we were working to help the shelter, they agreed to give us a grant—a gift of money we can use to keep the shelter open and running. Isn't that wonderful?"

Everyone cheered and then the twins were given the best reward of all. They fed all the new puppies—and got licked as a "thank-you."

52 Student Workbook

© Englefield & Associates, Inc.

Now answer Numbers 18 through 20 on your Reading Practice Tutorial Answer Sheet on page 56. Base your answers on the story "Funds for Food."

18 What is the primary reason Jeanette and Jessica walk Mrs. Cotton's dogs?

    F.   They enjoy working with animals.

    G.   They want to earn money for the shelter.

    H.   Mrs. Cotton is unable to walk her dogs.

    I.   They want to earn money to buy bicycles.

19 Which of the following was NOT a result of working to raise funds?

    A.   The shelter received several boxes of used blankets.

    B.   The City Council gave the shelter a grant.

    C.   The Snowden family purchased food for the shelter.

    D.   The volunteers were able to keep the shelter open.

20 What is Mrs. Snowden's reaction to her girls wanting to raise money?

    F.   She knows they usually do what they set out to do.

    G.   She worries that they might not be able to do it.

    H.   She thinks they are heading for trouble.

    I.   She believes that they will forget all about it.

This is the end of the Reading Practice Tutorial.
Until time is called, go back and check your work or answer questions you did not complete. When you have finished, close your workbook.

Answer Sheet

Practice Tutorial Answer Sheet

Answer all the questions that appear in the Practice Tutorial on this Answer Sheet. Answer each multiple-choice question by filling in the bubble for the answer you select.
To remove your Answer Sheet, carefully tear along the dotted line.

Name _____

Answer all questions that appear in the Reading Practice Tutorial on this Answer Sheet.

1   Ⓐ Ⓑ Ⓒ Ⓓ   14   Ⓕ Ⓖ Ⓗ Ⓘ

2   Ⓕ Ⓖ Ⓗ Ⓘ   15   Ⓐ Ⓑ Ⓒ Ⓓ

3   Ⓐ Ⓑ Ⓒ Ⓓ   16   Ⓕ Ⓖ Ⓗ Ⓘ

4   Ⓕ Ⓖ Ⓗ Ⓘ   17   Ⓐ Ⓑ Ⓒ Ⓓ

5   Ⓐ Ⓑ Ⓒ Ⓓ   18   Ⓕ Ⓖ Ⓗ Ⓘ

6   Ⓕ Ⓖ Ⓗ Ⓘ   19   Ⓐ Ⓑ Ⓒ Ⓓ

7   Ⓐ Ⓑ Ⓒ Ⓓ   20   Ⓕ Ⓖ Ⓗ Ⓘ

8   Ⓕ Ⓖ Ⓗ Ⓘ

9   Ⓐ Ⓑ Ⓒ Ⓓ

10 Ⓕ Ⓖ Ⓗ Ⓘ

11 Ⓐ Ⓑ Ⓒ Ⓓ

12 Ⓕ Ⓖ Ⓗ Ⓘ

13 Ⓐ Ⓑ Ⓒ Ⓓ

Fold and Tear Carefully Along Dotted Line.

Reading Assessment

Directions for Taking the Reading Assessment

This Assessment test contains nine passages and 50 questions. Some of the passages are fiction; others are nonfiction. Read each passage and the questions that follow carefully. You may look back at any passage as many times as you would like. If you are unsure of a question, you can move to the next question, and go back to the question you skipped later.

This test contains multiple-choice questions. Multiple-choice questions require you to select the best answer possible from four choices. Remember to read the questions and the answer choices carefully. Only one answer is correct. You will mark your answers on the Answer Sheet starting on page 98 of this workbook. Fill in the answer bubble to mark your selection.

Reading Assessment

Read the story "New Kid in Town" before answering Numbers 1 through 6.

New Kid in Town

Tony felt like the shortest boy in class, and to make matters worse, he was the new kid on the block! Making friends wasn't the easiest thing to do in a new school. His mother told him he would fit right in with the other children, but for some reason, he just wasn't sure.

During homeroom, a brown-haired boy wearing a gray T-shirt said, "Hi," to Tony, but none of the other kids seemed to notice him. When the teacher called out his last name, she mispronounced it, and everyone laughed. Tony lowered his head and stared at the top of his desk. He didn't want to see the kids laughing at him; the sound of their laughter was bad enough. The teacher began her morning lesson. Tony couldn't focus. "This couldn't move any slower," he thought to himself. Time slowly crept by. Every so often, Tony would peek up at the clock. He was careful not to let his eyes move off the desk for very long.

Tony wasn't sure of the new school's schedule, so the ringing lunchbell surprised him. The new student walked down the hall to his locker and put his books away. In the cafeteria, he went through the line and got his tray. He found a table near the window and sat alone. The air around him felt cold, unlike his old school which always felt warm and inviting. "If only I could go back to my old school," he wished to himself taking another bite of pizza. "I'd have all of my old friends, and everything would be back to normal," he thought.

Changing schools had been hard for Tony. His father had taken a new job halfway through the school year. Tony had to say goodbye to his friends, to his teachers, and to the only home he had ever known. Tony didn't want to finish his lunch. He knew as soon as he did, he would have to make his way to the playground. He would watch all the other kids have fun as he stood off to the side. "I wonder if I can sit here until it's time to go back to class," he thought.

Tony took a look out the window. A group of boys from homeroom was playing kickball on the playground. The lunch monitor strolled past Tony and gave him a look suggesting he had better move along soon. He finished his milk and got up to put away his trash. Tony put on his coat, shoved his hands deep into his pockets, and headed out to watch the crowd. He sought out a place by the fence and slumped down to sit on the ground. He kept his head buried.

Go On ▶

"Hey! Hey you!" At first Tony didn't realize the voice was calling out for him. "You're the new kid, aren't you?" the boy in the gray T-shirt shouted.

"Yeah, I'm Tony." He lifted his eyes and squinted as the sunlight hit his face. He expected the boy would mimic the homeroom teacher and would mispronounce his last name.

The boy ran to where Tony was sitting. "I'm Solomon, but everyone just calls me Solo. I'm going to play kickball with the other guys. We need another player to make the teams even. Do you know how to play kickball?"

"Yeah, sure," he replied.

"Great!" Solo said. Solo reached out his hand and pulled Tony to his feet. Tony realized he wasn't the shortest kid in class. He and Solo stood eye to eye. The boys ran toward the makeshift field. "Tony's gonna play," Solo yelled. Tony was worried someone would object, but the only words anyone uttered were, "Next up!"

Tony took his seat with his team. The boys started quizzing him on his old school and where he used to live. Everyone was interested in what he had to say, and he appreciated the attention. The kickball game ended with a winning run scored by Tony's team. As the boys celebrated, Tony realized being a new kid in town wasn't so bad after all.

Now answer Numbers 1 through 6 on your Reading Assessment Answer Sheet on page 98. Base your answers on the story "New Kid in Town."

1 Read this sentence from the story.

He expected the boy would mimic the homeroom teacher and would mispronounce his last name.

What does the word *mimic* mean?

A. misspell

B. misspeak

C. imitate ⏷

D. tease

2 What is the MAIN idea of the story?

F. Tony's family moves to a new neighborhood.

G. Tony wants to go back to his old school.

H. Tony plays kickball at the new school.

I. Tony doesn't think he'll make friends at his new school. ⏷

3 According to the story, Tony

A. is the shortest kid in school. ⏷

B. is happy to be at the new school.

C. is the same height as Solomon.

D. wears a gray T-shirt.

4 Read this sentence from the story.

Tony lowered his head and stared at the top of his desk.

Why does Tony stare at his desk?

F.   He can't read the board.

G.   He doesn't want to look at the kids who are laughing at him.

H.   He doesn't want to look out the window and see kids playing kickball.

I.   He wants to read a book instead of listening to the teacher's lesson.

5 As Tony sits in the cafeteria, he thinks

A.   his old school was more comforting.

B.   the new school is more inviting than his old school.

C.   the new school is warm.

D.   the old school cafeteria served better food.

6 Who helps solve Tony's problem?

F.   his mother

G.   his homeroom teacher

H.   Solomon

I.   his father

Read the articles "On the Hunt for a Fossil" and "A Modern-Day Fossilist's Checklist" before answering Numbers 7 through 14.

On the Hunt for a Fossil

Have you ever wanted to be a fossilist? Human beings have been searching for fossils for centuries. Fossilists are people who search for fossils. Fossils are the remains of centuries-old plants and animals that have been preserved. Fossils are oftentimes found in sedimentary rock. Sedimentary rock is formed when layers of dirt are compacted together. Examples of sedimentary rock include limestone, sandstone, and shale. Fossils have also been discovered in amber[1], ice, and asphalt[2]. Some of the oldest fossils can be as old as 3.5 billion years. Newer fossils are about 10,000 years old.

Paleontologists and fossilists are people who seek out and study fossils and other organic remains. They have gone all over the world looking for these rare relics. Fossils can be found around the globe, from Greenland to Antarctica and everywhere in between. Modern-day paleontologists carry special tools with them, including chipping hammers, chisels, collecting bags, gloves, eye protection, soft brushes, special maps and computers, and small shovels called trowels. They also bring along magnifying glasses so they can see tiny things more clearly. Most also carry notebooks for recording information.

Fossilists haven't always had the benefit of maps and special tools, however. Long ago, fossil hunters had to rely on their senses as well as on keen observation. One person known for her early fossil-hunting skills was Mary Anning. Born in 1799, Mary's family was very poor, especially after the death of her father in 1810. As a teenager, Mary would often walk the unstable cliffs near her home of Lyme Regis, England, in search of fossils. She collected fossils and sold them to scientists, to collectors, and to museums in order to make money. As her knowledge of fossils and their origins grew, she demonstrated talents as a well-skilled fossil hunter.

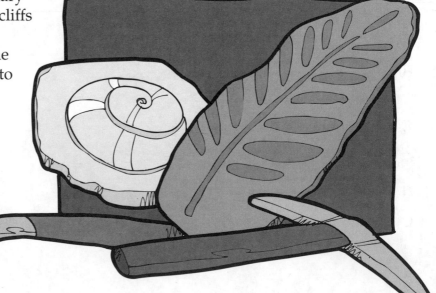

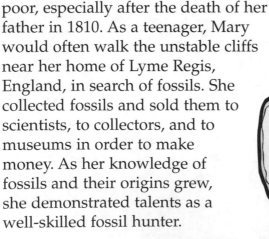

[1] **amber:** a yellowish-brown, see-through substance made of hardened sap
[2] **asphalt:** black, tar-like substance used for paving roads

Many scientists credit Mary with early discoveries of ichthyosaur and plesiosaurus fossils. Both finds were considered extremely important to the scientific community. Despite her refined talent, Mary had to sell her findings in order to survive. It wasn't until much later in her life that Mary's abilities were recognized. In 1838, she received wages from the British Association for the Advancement of Science. Around this time, she also received a stipend[3] from the Geological Society of London so she could pay her living expenses. Until her death in 1847, Mary, or "Fossil Woman" as she became known, searched for fossils. During her lifetime, she made important discoveries including the skeletons of sea serpents and flying dinosaurs.

Today, both professionals and beginners enjoy fossil hunting. Although it isn't easy, the search is exciting. Next time you're out in the back yard, be sure to take an extra close look at any rocks you find. Maybe you will be the next Mary Anning!

[3] **stipend:** wages; a salary

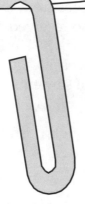

A Modern-Day Fossilist's Checklist

So you want to be a fossilist! Here are a few things every fossilist needs. Having the right tools and the right information is important, especially if you want to bring home more than a few broken stones. Remember to talk with your parents before you decide to do any work as a fossilist. There are many tools you will need their permission to use. After discussing this exciting hobby, maybe you'll get your mom and dad excited about fossils, too.

☐ Geologist's Rock Pick: the square end will break up rock, while the pick end will help you dig

☐ Chipping Hammer: this hammer has a flat blade that is useful for splitting or trimming rock

☐ Chisel: smaller than a chipping hammer, this tool comes in a variety of sizes; it is also good for splitting and trimming smaller rocks

☐ Safety Goggles & Gloves: important forms of protection when cutting rock

☐ Tweezers: very useful when removing very small pieces

☐ Trowel: helpful for digging soft earth

☐ Soft Brush: the brush will dust off your search site

☐ Compass: will help you find your way

☐ Maps: used to identify where you've been and where you're going

☐ Measurement Device: you many want to measure the size of your find

☐ Magnifying Glass: useful for looking at the smallest details

☐ Camera: you may want to take pictures of your find

☐ Notebook & Pencil: for taking notes

☐ Collecting Bags: plastic bags work just fine; use these to store your fossils

☐ Books & Other Resources: field guides will help you identify areas with many fossils; they may also help you identify what you have found; do some research on fossil hunting before you begin–they will discuss techniques for digging, searching, and collecting

Now answer Numbers 7 through 14 on your Reading Assessment Answer Sheet on page 98. Base your answers on the articles "On the Hunt for a Fossil" and "A Modern-Day Fossilist's Checklist."

7 Which of the following is NOT mentioned in the article as a place to find fossils?

A. ice

B. wood

C. amber

D. limestone

8 Why did the author write "On the Hunt for a Fossil"?

F. to discuss the work of fossilists

G. to tell the story of Mary Anning

H. to inform readers about the tools fossilists use

I. to give information about the age of fossils

9 Which of the following is NOT used for breaking a rock?

A. chipping hammer

B. rock pick

C. trowel

D. chisel

10 Why did Mary Anning first hunt for fossils?

   F.   The Geological Society of London paid her to look for fossils.

   G.   The British Association for the Advancement of Science wanted her to find fossils.

   H.   She sold the fossils she found in order to support her family.

   I.   She enjoyed discovering the fossils for private collection.

11 What was the primary tool used by Mary Anning as she looked for fossils?

   A.   a rock pick

   B.   a keen sense of observation

   C.   a magnifying glass

   D.   a computer

12 Why did the author write "A Modern-Day Fossilist's Checklist"?

   F.   to describe the tools a fossilist will need

   G.   to describe the types of rock picks used by fossilists

   H.   to tell the reader what to look for when searching for fossils

   I.   to entertain the reader with stories of fossil hunting

Go On ▶

13 Read this sentence from "On the Hunt for a Fossil."

   They have gone all over the world looking for these rare relics.

What is a *relic*?

   A.   an object from the past

   B.   a new object

   C.   the act of discovering

   D.   a tool used by fossilists

14 How are "On the Hunt for a Fossil" and "A Modern-Day Fossilist's Checklist" ALIKE?

   F.   They both give details about Mary Anning's life.

   G.   They both give a definition of a fossilist.

   H.   They both describe tools used by fossilists hundreds of years ago.

   I.   They both describe tools used by the fossilist.

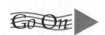

Read the story "Go West, I Say, Go West!" before answering Numbers 15 through 19.

Go West, I Say, Go West!

Slowly, the man walked down the dirt street, right through the middle of town. He knew everyone's eyes were on him as he strolled proudly toward the general store. Eyes peeked at him from second-story windows. There were multiple faces visible through every open doorway, and no one on the wooden sidewalks had moved a step since the man had appeared. His clothes and his walk told everyone he was a rich man—a rich man with something to say.

It seemed as though the entire town was holding its breath as he climbed up on the back of a wagon and called for everyone's attention. The words "General Store" loomed over his raised arms. Even the horse seemed to turn his head to the side so he could listen.

"Ladies and Gentlemen!" he cried out. "I am here today to ask you an important question. It's a simple question—one you probably have already asked yourself before."

In the small Eastern town, the only sounds heard were those of women's skirts rustling and of men's boots scraping, as people crowded closer to hear what the rich man was going to say next.

"The question is . . ." he paused, making sure that all eyes were looking at him, and only him.

"Are you happy? That's it. Are you happy?" He lowered his arms to his knees, bending them slightly. He looked at the eyes of the crowd, panning his gaze back and forth.

The crowd began to mumble softly; women whispering, men chuckling.

"Are you?" he asked again, raising his arms a second time and shouting more loudly than the first time. "Maybe you're just waiting and hoping for happiness? For a new start? For a new beginning? If you're tired of waiting and hoping, I have the answer for you! Get away from this dry place. Leave these harsh winters behind. Forget your barren fields and your tired forests."

The crowd's mumbling grew louder, and people began to move around, shifting from foot to foot. They were curious, anxious, and unsure all rolled into one.

"It's time for you to go west!" shouted the man. "Go west where you can have land to call your own. It's almost 1850, and the place to be is in California! Imagine a place where the land is so rich, you can grow anything. There are forests full of trees, and the hunting is plentiful! The weather is pleasant, and water is always close by. What are you waiting for?"

Voices could be heard now as people talked to each other and leaned to whisper in each other's ears. Was this the truth? Could the man be lying? But he was dressed so nicely.

Why hadn't they heard about the wonders of this new place until now? California was a site for gold rushers, but many of the townspeople had never heard of all the other pleasantries mentioned by the man.

"Almost a thousand people have already made the trip!" continued the man. "I'm here to make sure you STOP talking about it and START doing it. Saddle up your horses! Load up your wagons! Head out today on the California Trail! The first wagon train leaves tomorrow!"

"Wait a minute!" shouted a man from the front of the crowd. "Is California a state yet?"

"Just about!" replied the mysterious man. "It will happen before the year is out."

"I thought California was for just gold rushers," said a young man. Heads began to nod and murmurs of agreement were heard.

"Gold? Yes, of course there's gold!" he replied. "Rivers full of it, just waiting for you to find it and make your fortune."

"Is there enough good land for everyone?" asked a woman with a child on her hip.

"Ma'am, there's more land than they know what to do with. It's cheap land. Some of it is even free!" Excitement ran through the crowd now. The word "free" echoed among the whispers.

"Enough!" shouted the man and silence returned. "The first wagon train leaves tomorrow at noon. If you want to go, be here an hour earlier with your family and your belongings. Your future is waiting to begin!"

With that, the man jumped down from the wagon. Members of the crowd called out to him, but he let their questions sting his back as he walked away. By morning, half the town, with dreams of all-new beginnings on their minds, were lined up behind the rich man's wagon. With a crack of his reins, the wagon train began to move.

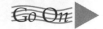

Now answer Numbers 15 through 19 on your Reading Assessment Answer Sheet on page 98. Base your answers on the story "Go West, I Say Go West!"

15 Read this sentence from the story.

> **Members of the crowd called out to him, but he let their questions sting his back as he walked away.**

According to this sentence,

A. the rich man ignored the people's questions.

B. the townspeople threw things at the rich man.

C. the rich man answered the people's questions.

D. the rich man threw things at members of the crowd.

16 According to the rich man, how is the West DIFFERENT from the Eastern town?

F. Land in the West is expensive because it is good for farming, while land in the East is cheap.

G. People are happier in the East.

H. The weather in the West is pleasant, while there are harsh winters in the East.

I. There are forests full of trees in the East, but in the West there is rich farmland.

17 Which event occurred LAST?

    A.   The rich man strolled into town.

    B.   The rich man led the wagon train.

    C.   The rich man strolled away from the crowd.

    D.   The rich man gave a speech about the wonders of the West.

18 Why did the man dress in nice clothes?

    F.   People were more likely to believe him if he dressed nicely.

    G.   He liked to dress in fancy clothes.

    H.   He lost his work clothes and had to wear nice clothes that day.

    I.   It was cold outside, and his nice clothes were warm.

19 Why did half the town decide to follow the rich man?

    A.   They wanted to work for the rich man.

    B.   The rich man promised a better life in the South.

    C.   They can't find work in the Eastern town.

    D.   The rich man promised a better life in the West.

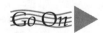

Read the poem "Could Not Wait" before answering Numbers 20 through 23.

COULD NOT WAIT

Sneaking through the mansion's gate,

my exploration could not wait.

From room to room, I gazed high, then low,

what I would find, I did not know.

The rooms were stark[1], the fixtures dark,

and I was all alone.

But not for long,

Something's wrong: the visitors are two;

if I'm caught—though I'd rather not—surely I'll be through!

In these few words he said to me,

"I wonder if you'll look at me."

I stopped and stared and did not know

the voice from a face that did not show.

I walked four steps and turned around;

there were no footsteps on the ground.

I slinked and crouched all through the hall,

but the voice shouted out: boy, stand up tall!

[1] **stark:** bare

Scared, I knew not what to do—
"House," I thought, "I'm through with you."

Quickly, I zipped passed a mirror,
when suddenly there was a cheer.

"You looked, you looked, you looked at me,"
the tall, framed mirror shouted out with glee.
Haunted by the ghostly shout,
I rushed to find my exit out.

Oh no, oh no, please, please don't go.
I promise I am not your foe.

Down the hall, and down the stairs,
I wonder why this mirror cares.

No time for that, don't want to chat.
I'll be gone in seconds flat.

I made it through the mansion's gate,
to get away, I could not wait.

Now answer Numbers 20 through 23 on your Reading Assessment Answer Sheet on page 98. Base your answers on the poem "Could Not Wait."

20 The narrator of this poem faces what problem?

    F.   He gets caught sneaking in an old mansion.

    G.   He is lost in an old mansion.

    H.√ He is scared by a mirror that talks to him.

    I.   He doesn't have a place to live.

21 Read this stanza from the poem.

    Oh no, oh no, please, please don't go.
    I promise I am not your foe.

What does the word *foe* mean?

    A.   friend

    B.√ enemy

    C.   ghost

    D.   stranger

22 Which words BEST describe the inside of the mansion?

    F.   bright; well-decorated

    G.   ugly; small

    H.√ unlit; empty

    I.   cheery; sunny

23 How does the narrator know he is NOT alone in the mansion?

    A.   He hears footsteps.

    B.√ He hears a voice.

    C.   Someone grabs his arm.

    D.   He sees someone.

Read the passage "Soccer" before answering Numbers 24 through 29.

Soccer is a popular sport played worldwide both professionally and for fun. In over 200 countries, soccer is played by people of all ages. Only in the United States is the game referred to as "soccer." In other parts of the world, it is referred to as football or fútbol.

Historians have found evidence that suggests ancient people made up and participated in different kicking games, similar to soccer. The game of soccer, as we know it today, however, began in England around the 19th century. Official rules were drafted for games involving ball handling in the late 1800s, and at that time, the game allowed for greater use of the hands than is permitted with modern soccer. A meeting of the London Football Association in 1863, however, split football into two sports. The first was rugby football, which is the parent sport of American football. This game allowed for touching and carrying the ball. The second sport was association football, or soccer, which did not allow the use of the hands.

Throughout the rest of the 1800s, soccer's popularity was widespread in England and Scotland. British traders, sailors, and soldiers carried the sport to Germany, Italy, Austria, and South America. In 1904, the Federation Internationale de Football Association (FIFA) was formed. FIFA is still the worldwide governing body of soccer. In 1930, FIFA organized the first World Cup, soccer's premier tournament which is held every four years.

Soccer was not always such a popular sport in America. While many other countries throughout Europe and South America embraced the game of soccer, it was slow to gain acceptance in the United States. It wasn't until the 1970s that the North American Soccer League gained the interest of fans in the United States. Although the league eventually went out of business because of financial problems, it left a lasting impression on Americans, particularly among young people. Today, soccer is the fastest-growing high school and college sport in the United States.

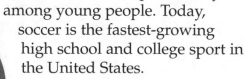

Now answer Numbers 24 through 29 on your Reading Assessment Answer Sheet on pages 98–99. Base your answers on the passage "Soccer."

24 The author's purpose in writing this passage is to

    F.   entertain the reader with stories about soccer.

    G.   give the reader information about the game of soccer.

    H.   persuade readers to learn to play soccer.

    I.   remind readers to watch soccer on television.

25 According to the passage, citizens of which country FIRST played soccer as we know it?

    A.   Greece

    B.   Italy

    C.   England

    D.   United States

26 The author of this passage gives you reason to believe

    F.   soccer has always been a popular sport in the United States.

    G.   soccer was not always popular in the United States.

    H.   football replaced soccer in England.

    I.   soccer was first played in the United States.

27 How are rugby football and association football DIFFERENT?

    A.   Players use their hands for association football, but not for rugby football.

    B.   Rugby football is the parent sport of soccer, while association football is the parent sport of American football.

    C.   Each was created at a meeting of the London Football Association in 1863.

    D.   Rugby football is the parent sport of American football, while association football is the parent sport of soccer.

28 Read this sentence from the passage.

> **While many other countries throughout Europe and South America embraced the game of soccer, it was slow to gain acceptance in the United States.**

What word has the same meaning as *embraced*?

F. accepted

G. ignored

H. hugged

I. feared

29 With which statement would the author of this passage MOST likely disagree?

A. Forms of soccer have been played all over the world for hundreds of years.

B. Soccer is no longer popular in England.

C. Soccer is gaining popularity in the United States.

D. The North American Soccer League helped the growth of soccer in the United States.

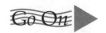

Read the passage "Summer Fun Camp" before answering Numbers 30 through 34.

Summer Fun Camp

Every day, Samantha stared out the front window at 10:00 a.m. That's when the mailman slowly pulled his truck up to the mailbox and dropped off the Perkins' mail. As soon as the white square vehicle headed to the next house, Samantha was out the door. She rushed down the brick sidewalk, swung open the white picket fence, and pulled down the mailbox door. She would examine the contents as she made her way back to the house. Each day, for the past five, she found nothing with her name on it. This day was different, however. The inside of the mailbox was crowded. A large, brown envelope took up most of the space inside the metal box. She tugged at the stack of mail, freeing the envelope, her envelope. The label on the front read: Samantha Perkins.

Finally, the information packet from the Hillsboro Summer Fun Camp had arrived. She had been expecting this bundle for a week. Samantha couldn't wait to get inside. She wanted to tear into the brown paper right there in the front yard, but it was windy and she didn't want to lose any of the information.

She rushed to the house and made her way to the kitchen. She opened the envelope and carefully laid out its contents on the table. She found a welcome letter, a daily program, and a list of activities. Samantha was a little nervous about going to a place so far away, but once she saw all the activities, she knew it would be fun. As she looked through each piece, she started to daydream about summer camp.

Dear Hillsboro Summer Fun Camp Camper:

Congratulations on your decision to attend the Hillsboro Summer Fun Camp! We are excited to have you as a special guest. The Hillsboro Camp is 14 days long, and you are scheduled to arrive Saturday, July 3. Mark your calendar!

While at camp, you will have the opportunity to try new and exciting activities. A complete list of the activities is provided for you. Look through this list. Please let someone at Hillsboro Camp know if you are unable to participate in any of these activities.

Feel free to contact us if you have any questions. We look forward to meeting you this July 3.

See you soon!

Hillsboro Summer Fun Camp Counselors

Go On

Hillsboro Summer Fun

Daily Camp Schedule

Breakfast	7:30 a.m. – 8:30 a.m.
Morning Activity	8:30 a.m. – Noon
Lunch	Noon – 1:00 p.m.
Afternoon Activity	1:00 p.m. – 4:30 p.m.
Free Time	4:30 p.m. – 5:30 p.m.
Dinner	5:30 p.m. – 6:30 p.m.
Campfire	6:30 p.m. – 8:30 p.m.
Lights Out	10:00 p.m

Hillsboro Summer Fun

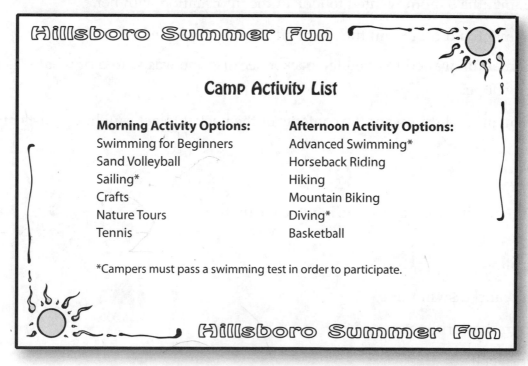

Hillsboro Summer Fun

Camp Activity List

Morning Activity Options:
Swimming for Beginners
Sand Volleyball
Sailing*
Crafts
Nature Tours
Tennis

Afternoon Activity Options:
Advanced Swimming*
Horseback Riding
Hiking
Mountain Biking
Diving*
Basketball

*Campers must pass a swimming test in order to participate.

Hillsboro Summer Fun

Now answer Numbers 30 through 34 on your Reading Assessment Answer Sheet on page 99. Base your answers on the passage "Summer Fun Camp."

30 If Samantha wants to participate in sailing, what must she do?

    F. She must take a beginner's course for sailing.

    G. She must pass the swimming test.

    H. She must pass the sailing test.

    I. She must get permission from the sailing instructor.

31 Why did Samantha wait until she was in the kitchen to open her packet from Hillsboro?

    A. Samantha's mom wanted to look at the information with her.

    B. Samantha didn't want the mailman to look at her packet.

    C. Samantha waited to open the packet because she was scared of what was inside the envelope.

    D. Samantha didn't want the contents of the packet to get caught by gusts of wind.

32 Samantha will NOT participate in which activity?

    F. sailing

    G. advanced swimming

    H. horseback riding

    I. baseball

33 Which of the following might be the correct order for part of Samantha's schedule on her second day at camp?

    A. breakfast, sand volleyball, lunch, diving

    B. hiking, lunch, crafts, free time

    C. free time, hiking, dinner, campfire

    D. breakfast, horseback riding, lunch, tennis

34 Which of the following describes how Samantha feels about camp?

    F. She is scared because she doesn't know anyone at the camp.

    G. She is afraid because she doesn't know how to swim.

    H. She is nervous because it is far away, but she is excited about all the activities.

    I. She doesn't have any fears at all, and she is excited about attending camp.

Read the story "Summer Fun" before answering Numbers 35 through 40.

Summer Fun

"Wake up!" Meredith shouted at her brother, who was still asleep. "Today is the first day of summer vacation!" Meredith was anxious to start summer fun, but her brother had no interest in anything other than crawling under his soft sheets. Max mumbled something impossible to hear and rolled back over, pulling the comforter over his head.

"Mom says we can go to the wave pool if all our chores are done," Meredith said trying to convince Max to get out of bed. "Mine are done, so get dressed and get moving. I want to get to the wave pool." She shut his bedroom door and skipped downstairs.

Meredith had been up since the crack of dawn. Summer held so many possibilities for fun; she couldn't wait to get started. Her bed was made; her floor was spotless. Her fifth-grade schoolbooks had been lined up neatly on the shelf. After finding a spot in her closet for her backpack, all Meredith could think about was summer fun. Her daydream was interrupted by a phone call. Meredith dashed into the kitchen to answer it: "Marshall residence."

"Hello. This is Amy. Is Meredith home?"

Meredith and Amy had been best friends since first grade and lived in the same neighborhood just two blocks from each other.

"Hi, Amy! Can you believe it's really summer?"

"What do you want to do today?" Meredith asked. "I was thinking about going to the wave pool. Do you want to go with us?"

"Cool. Let me check with my mom." Amy cupped her hand over the phone. "MOMMM!" she hollered. Even though the phone was covered, Meredith could still hear the voice. "Can I go to the wave pool with Meredith?"

Copying is Prohibited
© Englefield & Associates, Inc.

Amy knew what the response would be. Her room was a disaster area. Clothes had been thrown on the floor, her backpack and books were spread out on the desk, and CDs were scattered across the bed.

She came back to the phone with a response. "I can't go until my room is picked up," Amy said, "and it's a real mess!"

"How long do you think you'll be?" Meredith asked.

"Well, I think I can get it finished before you leave for the pool," Amy answered, mentally plotting where she could throw all her stuff—under the bed, her closet, her drawers—her favorite hiding spots. "I can sort it all out later," she thought to herself.

Meredith knew better; she knew what Amy was planning. Amy was not tidy. She was the messiest person Meredith knew, and if the girls wanted to get to the wave pool, Amy was going to need some help. "Amy, if you don't really clean your room today, you're going to have to face it another day. You'll probably spend most of the summer trying to get your room in order. I'll help you with your room today, and you can help me with some chores later this week. How's that sound?"

"Great!" Amy said excitedly. She knew Meredith was right, and she was grateful for some assistance. Amy was nothing like her neat and tidy best friend. In order to have any fun this summer, she needed to silence her mom's groans about a sloppy room. Luckily, Meredith was always there to help.

Go On ▶

Now answer Numbers 35 through 40 on your Reading Assessment Answer Sheet on page 99. Base your answers on the story "Summer Fun."

35 Which of these BEST describes Meredith?

    A. careless

    B. helpful

    C. clumsy

    D. tired

36 What is the MAIN problem Meredith faces in the story?

    F. Meredith's brother and her friend have chores to finish before they can go to the pool.

    G. Meredith's brother is still asleep, so they can't go to the pool.

    H. Amy isn't allowed to go to the pool with Meredith.

    I. Meredith's mom is at work and can't take her and Amy to the pool.

37 Why did the author title the story "Summer Fun"?

    A. The author thinks chores are fun.

    B. The author wants readers to know summer is the only fun time of year.

    C. The author wants to let readers know why Meredith is excited about summer.

    D. The author thinks Meredith is the only who is going to have a fun summer.

38 What step does Meredith take when trying to solve the problem she faces?

    F.   She tells her mom she is going to Amy's house, but she goes to the wave pool instead.

    G.   She promises Amy's mom that she will clean Amy's room another day.

    H.   She offers to help Amy clean her room.

    I.   She offers to do her brother's chores.

39 How is Meredith's room DIFFERENT from Amy's room?

    A.   Amy's room is neat, while Meredith's room is a mess.

    B.   Amy stacked her schoolbooks on her shelf, and Meredith put her schoolbooks in her closet.

    C.   Meredith's room is bright and sunny, but Amy's room is dark.

    D.   Meredith has everything put away, but Amy has things thrown all over her room.

40 Which statement about Meredith and Max is MOST accurate?

    F.   Meredith is excited to start summer activities, and Max isn't interested.

    G.   Meredith likes to keep her room clean, and so does Max.

    H.   Meredith and Max share a bedroom.

    I.   Meredith and Max are both excited about going to the wave pool.

Read the article "Giraffes" before answering Numbers 41 through 45.

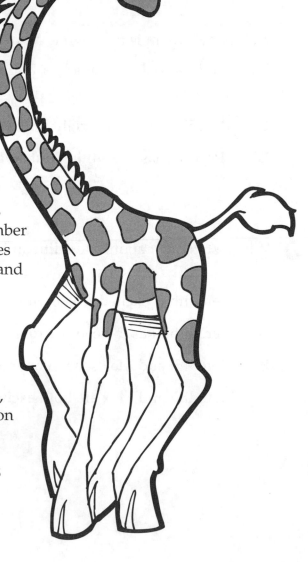

The word giraffe comes from an Arabic word *zirafah*, which means the tallest of all. Giraffes are the tallest of all mammals. In fact, a newborn giraffe is about six feet tall when it is born. That's taller than the height of an average human adult! Adult female giraffes, called cows, can be over 16 feet tall. Adult male giraffes, called bulls, can be over 18 feet tall. While most people are familiar with a giraffe's height, they might be surprised to hear about its weight. An adult male giraffe can weigh up to 4,400 pounds. That's 1.5 tons! This makes the giraffe one of the heaviest land animals on Earth today.

The neck of an adult giraffe is just over five feet long. Even though its neck is very long, the giraffe's neck has only seven vertebrae. This is the same number found in other mammals, including humans. Giraffes have long legs with hoofs the size of dinner plates, and can run up to 35 miles per hour.

These tall animals live in open woodland and wooded grasslands throughout eastern and southern Africa, where they eat leaves off trees. Their favorite leaves are those of Acacia trees. Although giraffes eat mostly tree shoots and leaves, they also eat flowers, vines, and herbs, depending on the season of the year. The animals use their long, black tongues to pull the leaves off the tree. Their tongues are like hands and are on average about 18 inches long.

Go On ▶

Each adult giraffe eats up to 75 pounds of leaves a day. Thus, these animals spend most of their time feeding; an average of 16 to 20 hours per day. Because of the need for so many leaves, giraffe herds can be spread out as far as a half-mile. How could each giraffe be sure to get enough leaves if they all stood close together? Giraffes have excellent eyesight. Since they are very tall, giraffes can see for miles, far better than other animals.

In addition, giraffes are so large that other animals usually do not try to attack them. That is why the herd can spread apart to feed. Giraffes drink water if it is available but can go weeks without it. Otherwise, they rely on the morning dew and the water content of their food. At a water hole, up to 12 gallons at a time may be taken in by one giraffe.

Of course, giraffes do have predators. Their main predators are humans. Giraffes are hunted for their hides and hair as well as for their tough but healthy meat. Laws now forbid the hunting of giraffes in the wild. The giraffe's other main predators are lions, hyenas, and leopards. Lions generally attack young calves because an adult giraffe can defend itself by kicking and, if necessary, can usually outrun a lion. To protect her calf from a lion attack, a mother giraffe stands over her young. When there is no threat of attack, a mother giraffe hides her young or leaves them with other cows.

The herd that is composed of cows and their offspring is only one type of giraffe herd. Other herds include all females, all males, or males and females of all ages. Still, not all giraffes live in herds. For example, a bull looking for a mate, or a cow protecting her newborn, might live alone.

Giraffes have a yellow-colored coat splashed with irregular brown to rich chestnut patches that look like puzzle pieces. The markings of each giraffe, like the fingerprints of each human, are unique. There are eight known varieties, or races, of giraffes, which can be identified by the markings or patterns of their coats. Both sexes have knobby horns of solid bones and skin. Giraffes can live to be 20 to 25 years old.

Now answer Numbers 41 through 45 on your Reading Assessment Answer Sheet on page 99. Base your answers on the article "Giraffes."

41 Which of the following BEST represents the main idea of the first paragraph?

    A. Giraffes are very heavy mammals.

    B. Giraffes are very smart mammals.

    C. Giraffes are very tall mammals.

    D. Giraffes are mammals.

42 Based on the information from the article, which statement is TRUE?

    F. All giraffes live in herds for protection.

    G. Giraffes have no natural enemies.

    H. Giraffes do not live in herds; because of their height, they can see predators from great distances.

    I. A female giraffe protects her young by standing over it.

43 Laws have been created to protect giraffes from

    A. lions.

    B. pollution.

    C. hunters.

    D. zoos.

44 What is the author's MAIN purpose in writing "Giraffes"?

    F.   to inform readers about giraffes

    G.   to persuade readers to protect giraffes

    H.   to express an opinion on conserving woodlands

    I.   to entertain readers with a safari passage

45 According to the article, where would you MOST likely find giraffes living in the wild?

    A.   North American tundra

    B.   tropical forests in South America

    C.   woodlands of eastern Africa

    D.   mountain ranges of the Asia

Read the story "The Little Glass Slipper" before answering Numbers 46 through 50.

The Little Glass Slipper

"Come, child," said the Godmother, "or you will be late."

As Cinderella moved, the light shone upon her dainty shoes.

"They are of diamonds," she said.

"No," answered her Godmother, smiling; "they are better than that—they are of glass, made by the fairies. And now, child, go, and enjoy yourself."

But her Godmother, above all things, told her not to stay till after midnight, telling her at the same time that if she stayed one moment longer, the coach would be a pumpkin again, her horses mice, her coachman a rat, her footmen lizards, and her clothes would become just as they were before.

She promised her Godmother she would not fail to leave the ball before midnight.

At the ball, the King's son was always by her side. All this was so far from being tiresome that she quite forgot what her Godmother had told her. She at last counted the clock striking twelve when she took it to be no more than eleven. She then rose up and fled as nimble as a deer. The Prince followed, but could not catch her. She left behind one of her glass slippers, which the Prince took up most carefully.

On the following morning, there was a great noise of trumpets and drums, and a procession passed through the town, at the head of which rode the King's son. Behind him came a herald, bearing a velvet cushion, upon which rested a little glass slipper. The herald blew a blast upon the trumpet, and then read a proclamation saying that the King's son would wed any lady in the land who could fit the slipper upon her foot, if she could produce another to match it.

Go On ▶

Of course, the sisters tried to squeeze their feet into the slipper, but it was of no use—they were much too large. Then Cinderella shyly begged that she might try. How the sisters laughed with scorn when the Prince knelt to fit the slipper on the cinder maid's foot; but what was their surprise when it slipped on with the greatest ease, and the next moment Cinderella produced the other from her pocket! Once more she stood in the slippers, and once more the sisters saw before them the lovely Princess who was to be the Prince's bride. For at the touch of the magic shoes, the little gray frock disappeared forever, and in place of it she wore the beautiful robe the fairy Godmother had given to her.

So the poor little cinder maid married the Prince, and in time they came to be King and Queen, and lived happily ever after.

Now answer Numbers 46 through 50 on your Reading Assessment Answer Sheet on page 99. Base your answers on the article "The Little Glass Slipper."

46 What problem does Cinderella face?

    F.   She can't make the Prince fall in love with her.

    G.   She doesn't have anything to wear to the ball.

    H.   Her carriage turns into a pumpkin and she doesn't know how to get home.

    I.   She forgets to watch the clock and must run away from the Prince.

47 Why does the Prince marry Cinderella?

    A.   He finds out that she is a very fast runner.

    B.   The glass slipper fits her foot, and she has the other slipper.

    C.   She is friends with her fairy Godmother.

    D.   Her sisters tell the Prince that Cinderella is a nice girl and a hard worker.

48 What is the author's MAIN purpose in writing "The Little Glass Slipper"?

    F.   to entertain the reader with a story about an ordinary girl who marries a prince

    G.   to persuade the reader to watch the clock when you must be somewhere at a certain time

    H.   to inform the reader about how princes chose wives in medieval times

    I.   to explain how fairy Godmothers can make wishes come true

49 Read this sentence from the story.

> **As Cinderella moved, the light shone upon her dainty shoes.**

What does the word *dainty* mean?

A. light

B. broken

C. delicate

D. strong

50 After Cinderella promised her Godmother she would be home by midnight, what did Cinderella do next?

F. She put on the glass slippers.

G. She spent the evening with the Prince.

H. She pulled one glass slipper from her pocket.

I. She fled the ball.

This is the end of the Reading Assessment.
Until time is called, go back and check your work or answer questions you did not complete. When you have finished, close your workbook.

Answer Sheet

Reading Assessment Answer Sheet

Answer all the questions that appear in the Reading Assessment on this Answer Sheet.
Answer each multiple-choice question by filling in the bubble for the answer you select.
To remove your Answer Sheet, carefully tear along the dotted line.

Name _____

Answer all questions that appear in the Reading Practice Tutorial on this Answer Sheet.

1 Ⓐ Ⓑ Ⓒ Ⓓ   14 Ⓕ Ⓖ Ⓗ Ⓘ

2 Ⓕ Ⓖ Ⓗ Ⓘ   15 Ⓐ Ⓑ Ⓒ Ⓓ

3 Ⓐ Ⓑ Ⓒ Ⓓ   16 Ⓕ Ⓖ Ⓗ Ⓘ

4 Ⓕ Ⓖ Ⓗ Ⓘ   17 Ⓐ Ⓑ Ⓒ Ⓓ

5 Ⓐ Ⓑ Ⓒ Ⓓ   18 Ⓕ Ⓖ Ⓗ Ⓘ

6 Ⓕ Ⓖ Ⓗ Ⓘ   19 Ⓐ Ⓑ Ⓒ Ⓓ

7 Ⓐ Ⓑ Ⓒ Ⓓ   20 Ⓕ Ⓖ Ⓗ Ⓘ

8 Ⓕ Ⓖ Ⓗ Ⓘ   21 Ⓐ Ⓑ Ⓒ Ⓓ

9 Ⓐ Ⓑ Ⓒ Ⓓ   22 Ⓕ Ⓖ Ⓗ Ⓘ

10 Ⓕ Ⓖ Ⓗ Ⓘ   23 Ⓐ Ⓑ Ⓒ Ⓓ

11 Ⓐ Ⓑ Ⓒ Ⓓ   24 Ⓕ Ⓖ Ⓗ Ⓘ

12 Ⓕ Ⓖ Ⓗ Ⓘ   25 Ⓐ Ⓑ Ⓒ Ⓓ

13 Ⓐ Ⓑ Ⓒ Ⓓ   26 Ⓕ Ⓖ Ⓗ Ⓘ

Name _____

Answer all questions that appear in the Reading Assessment on this Answer Sheet.

27 Ⓐ Ⓑ © Ⓓ   39 Ⓐ Ⓑ © Ⓓ

28 Ⓕ Ⓖ Ⓗ Ⓘ   40 Ⓕ Ⓖ Ⓗ Ⓘ

29 Ⓐ Ⓑ © Ⓓ   41 Ⓐ Ⓑ © Ⓓ

30 Ⓕ Ⓖ Ⓗ Ⓘ   42 Ⓕ Ⓖ Ⓗ Ⓘ

31 Ⓐ Ⓑ © Ⓓ   43 Ⓐ Ⓑ © Ⓓ

32 Ⓕ Ⓖ Ⓗ Ⓘ   44 Ⓕ Ⓖ Ⓗ Ⓘ

33 Ⓐ Ⓑ © Ⓓ   45 Ⓐ Ⓑ © Ⓓ

34 Ⓕ Ⓖ Ⓗ Ⓘ   46 Ⓕ Ⓖ Ⓗ Ⓘ

35 Ⓐ Ⓑ © Ⓓ   47 Ⓐ Ⓑ © Ⓓ

36 Ⓕ Ⓖ Ⓗ Ⓘ   48 Ⓕ Ⓖ Ⓗ Ⓘ

37 Ⓐ Ⓑ © Ⓓ   49 Ⓐ Ⓑ © Ⓓ

38 Ⓕ Ⓖ Ⓗ Ⓘ   50 Ⓕ Ⓖ Ⓗ Ⓘ

Fold and Tear Carefully Along Dotted Line.

BLANK PAGE

Mathematics

Introduction

In the Mathematics section of the Florida Comprehensive Assessment Test (FCAT), you will be asked questions designed to test what you have learned in school. These questions have been written based on the mathematics you have been taught in school through fifth grade. The questions you answer are not meant to confuse or to trick you but are written so you have the best opportunity to show what you know about mathematics.

The *Show What You Know® on the 5th Grade FCAT, Student Workbook* includes a Mathematics Practice Tutorial that will help you practice your test-taking skills. Following the Mathematics Practice Tutorial is a full-length Mathematics Assessment. Both the Mathematics Practice Tutorial and the Mathematics Assessment have been created to model the fifth-grade FCAT.

About the FCAT Mathematics for Grade 5

Items in this section of the FCAT will test your ability to perform mathematical tasks in real-world and mathematical situations, and will neither require you to define mathematical terminology nor memorize specific facts. The FCAT is meant to gauge your ability to apply mathematical concepts to a given situation.

Item Distribution and Scoring

The following chart shows the approximate percent of raw-score points taken from each Mathematics Content Category.

Mathematics Content Categories	Points
Number Sense, Concepts, and Operations	20%
Measurement	20%
Geometry and Spacial Sense	20%
Algebraic Thinking	20%
Data Analysis	20%

The FCAT Mathematics will ask multiple-choice, gridded-response, short-response, and extended-response questions.

Mathematics Item Type	Number of Items
Multiple Choice	35–40
Gridded Response	10–15
Short and Extended Response	5–8
Total	50–55

Multiple-Choice Questions

On the fifth-grade FCAT, you will select from four possible answer choices and fill in a bubble in this workbook. Although multiple-choice items sometimes ask for the recall of facts, most of the sample items demand a more complex thought process. Each multiple-choice item on the assessment is scored 0 (incorrect) or 1 (correct). Each correct answer adds one point to your total assessment score.

Gridded-Response Questions

Each gridded-response question requires a numerical answer which should be filled into a bubble grid. The bubble grid consists of 4 columns. Each column contains numbers 0–9. Some grids may contain a column that shows only a decimal point. These grids allow you to enter answers that contain a decimal point. You do not need to include any commas for numbers greater than 999. When filling in your answer, you should only fill in one bubble per column. All gridded-response questions are constructed so the answer will fit into the grid. You can print your answer with the first digit in the left answer box, or with the last digit in the right answer box. Print only one digit or symbol in each answer box. Do not leave a blank box in the middle of an answer. Make sure to fill in a bubble under each box in which there is an answer and be sure to write the answer in the grid above the bubbles as well, in case clarification is needed. Answers can be given in whole number, percent, or decimal form. For questions involving measurements, the unit of measure required for the answer will be provided. When a percent is required to answer a question, do NOT convert the percent to its decimal or fractional equivalent. Grid in the percent value without the % symbol. If the answer is a mixed number, such as $13\frac{1}{4}$, convert the answer to a decimal number, in this case 13.25. You will also be instructed when to round your answer in a particular way. Some example responses are given below.

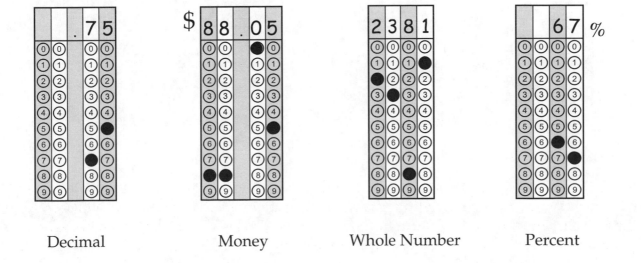

Decimal   Money   Whole Number   Percent

Short-Response Questions

Short-response items require you to generate your own answers—anything from a few words or numbers to several sentences. Many of these items ask you to explain your reasoning to support your answer. Short-response items are worth 2 points each and are scored according to the 2-point rubric below.

	Two-Point Rubric for Short-Response Tasks
2 points	A score of 2 indicates that the student has demonstrated a thorough understanding of the mathematics concepts and/or procedures embodied in the task. The student has completed the task correctly, in a mathematically sound manner. When required, student explanations and/or interpretations are clear and complete. The response may contain minor flaws that do not detract from the demonstration of a thorough understanding.
1 point	A score of 1 indicates that the student has provided a response that is only partially correct. For example, the student may provide a correct solution, but may demonstrate some misunderstanding of the underlying mathematical concepts or procedures. Conversely, a student may provide a computationally incorrect solution but could have applied appropriate and mathematically sound procedures, or the student's explanation could indicate an understanding of the task, despite the error.
0 points	A score of 0 indicates the student has provided either no response at all, or a completely incorrect or uninterpretable response, or demonstrated insufficient understanding of the mathematics concepts and/or procedures embodied in the task. For example, a student may provide some work that is mathematically correct, but the work does not demonstrate even a rudimentary understanding of the primary focus of the task.

Extended-Response Questions

Extended-response items require a more developed response and may ask for an essay on a single topic or several short paragraphs in response to individual items. Virtually every extended-response item will demand higher-level thinking skills. Many students offer very minimal written responses (3 words instead of 3 paragraphs). Good performance requires practice in writing full, well-supported responses. Extended-response items are worth 4 points each and are scored according to the 4-point rubric below.

	Four-Point Rubric for Extended-Response Tasks
4 points	A score of 4 is a response in which the student demonstrates a thorough understanding of the mathematics concepts and/or procedures embodied in the task. The student has responded correctly to the task, used mathematically sound procedures, and provided clear and complete explanations and interpretations. The response may contain minor flaws that do not detract from the demonstration of a thorough understanding.
3 points	A score of 3 is a response in which the student demonstrates an understanding of the mathematics concepts and/or procedures embodied in the task. The student's response to the task is essentially correct with the mathematical procedures used and the explanations and interpretations provided, demonstrating an essential, but less than thorough, understanding. The response may contain minor flaws that reflect inattentive execution of mathematical procedures or indications of some misunderstanding of the underlying mathematics concepts and/or procedures.
2 points	A score of 2 indicates that the student has demonstrated only a partial understanding of the mathematics concepts and/or procedures embodied in the task. Although the student may have used the correct approach to obtaining a solution or may have provided a correct solution, the student's work lacks an essential understanding of the underlying mathematical concepts. The response contains errors related to misunderstanding important aspects of the task, misuse of mathematical procedures, or faulty interpretations of results.
1 points	A score of 1 indicates that the student has demonstrated a very limited understanding of the mathematics concepts and/or procedures embodied in the task. The student's response is incomplete and exhibits many flaws. Although the student's response has addressed some of the conditions of the task, the student reached an inadequate conclusion and/or provided reasoning that was faulty or incomplete. The response exhibits many flaws or may be incomplete.
0 points	A score of 0 indicates the student has provided either no response at all, or a completely incorrect or uninterpretable response, or demonstrated insufficient understanding of the mathematics concepts and/or procedures embodied in the task. For example, a student may provide some work that is mathematically correct, but the work does not demonstrate even a rudimentary understanding of the primary focus of the task.

"Think, Solve, Explain" Questions

This symbol appears next to questions that require short written answers. Use about 5 minutes to answer these questions. A complete and correct answer to each of these questions is worth 2 points. A partially correct answer is worth 1 point:

This symbol appears next to questions that require longer written answers. Use about 10 to 15 minutes to answer these questions. A complete and correct answer to each of these questions is worth 4 points. A partially correct answer is worth 1, 2, or 3 points.

How to Answer the "Think, Solve, Explain" Questions

Answers to the short- and extended-response problems can receive full or partial credit. You should try to answer these questions even if you are not sure of the correct answer. If a portion of the answer is correct, you will get a portion of the points.

- Allow about 5 minutes to answer the short "Think, Solve, Explain" questions and about 10 to 15 minutes to answer the long questions.

- Read the question carefully.

- If you do not understand the question, read and answer one part at a time.

- Be sure to answer every part of the question.

- Use numbers and other information from the problem to answer the question.

- Show your work. This shows that you understand how to solve the problem.

- Write your explanations in clear, concise language.

- Check your work to make sure the procedure and calculations are correct.

- Reread your explanation to make sure it says what you want it to say.

Hints to Remember for Taking the FCAT Mathematics Test

Here are some hints to help you do your best when you take the FCAT Mathematics test. Keep these hints in mind when you answer the questions in the Mathematics Practice Tutorial and Mathematics Assessment.

- Read each problem carefully and think about ways to solve the problem before you try to answer the question.

- Answer the questions you are sure about first. If a question seems too difficult, skip it and go back to it later.

- Be sure to fill in the answer bubbles correctly. Do not make any stray marks around answer spaces.

- Think positively. Some problems may seem hard to you, but you may be able to figure out what to do if you read each question carefully.

- When you have finished each problem, reread it to make sure your answer is reasonable.

- Check each answer to make sure it is the best answer for the question asked.

- Relax. Some people get nervous about tests. It's natural. Just do your best.

Glossary

acute angle: An angle that measures less than 90 degrees and greater than 0 degrees.

addend: Numbers added together to give a sum. For example, in the equation 2 + 7 = 9, the numbers 2 and 7 are addends.

addition: An operation joining two or more sets where the result is the whole.

algebraic equation (inequality): A mathematical sentence that may contain variables, constants, and operation symbols in which two expressions are connected by an equality (or inequality) symbol.

algebraic expression: An expression containing numbers and variables (e.g., $7x$), and operations that involve numbers and variables (e.g., $2x + y$). Algebraic expressions may or may not contain equality or inequality symbols.

algebraic order of operations: The order in which computations are made in an algebraic expression. The order is: parentheses, multiplication/division (from left to right), addition/subtraction (from left to right).

algebraic rule: A mathematical expression containing variables and describing a pattern or relationship.

A.M.: The hours from midnight to noon; from Latin words *ante meridiem* meaning before noon.

analyze: To break down information into parts so that it may be more easily understood.

angle: A figure formed by two rays that meet at the same end point called a vertex. Angles can be obtuse, acute, right, or straight, and are measured in degrees.

area: The number of square units needed to cover the inside region of a closed two-dimensional figure. The most common abbreviation for area is A.

Associative Property of Addition: The grouping of addends can be changed and the sum will be the same. Example: (3 + 1) + 2 = 6; 3 + (1 + 2) = 6.

Associative Property of Multiplication: The grouping of factors can be changed and the product will be the same. Example: (3 x 2) x 4 = 24; 3 x (2 x 4) = 24.

attribute: A characteristic or distinctive feature.

average: A number found by adding two or more quantities together and then dividing the sum by the number of quantities. For example, in the set {9, 5, 4}, the average is 6: 9 + 5 + 4 = 18; 18 ÷ 3 = 6. *See mean.*

axes: Plural of axis. Perpendicular lines used as reference lines in a coordinate plane system or graph; traditionally, the horizontal axis (*x*-axis) represents the independent variable and the vertical axis (*y*-axis) represents the dependent variable.

bar graph: A graph using either vertical or horizontal bars to show data.

base (geometric): Usually refers to the side of a polygon closest to the bottom of the page. It is from the base that height can be measured.

break: A zigzag or v-shape on the *x*- or *y*-axis in a line or bar graph that indicates the data being displayed does not include all of the values that exist in the number line used. Breaks are very useful when there is a large difference between high and low values in the data set, or when specific values need to be excluded from the scale. Also called a squiggle.

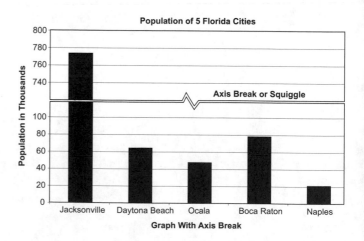

capacity: The amount an object holds when filled.

chart: A way to show information, such as in a graph or table.

Glossary

circle: Closed, curved line made up of points that are all the same distance from a point inside called the center. Example: A circle with center point P is shown below.

circle graph: Sometimes called a pie chart; a way of representing data that shows the fractional part or percentage of an overall set as an appropriately-sized wedge of a circle. Example:

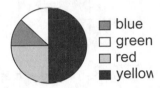

- ■ blue
- □ green
- ▨ red
- ■ yellow

circumference: The boundary line or perimeter of a circle; also, the length of the perimeter of a circle. Example:

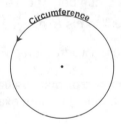

closed figure: A two-dimensional figure that divides the plane where the figure lies into two parts—the part inside the figure and the part outside the figure (e.g., circles, squares, triangles).

Commutative Property of Addition: Numbers can be added in any order and the sum will be the same. Example: 3 + 4 = 4 + 3.

Commutative Property of Multiplication: Numbers can be multiplied in any order and the product will be the same. Example: 3 x 6 = 6 x 3.

compare: To look for similarities and differences. For example, is one number greater than, less than, or equal to another number?

composite number: A number that has more than two factors. Examples include 4, 35, and 121. The numbers zero and one are not composite numbers.

conclusion: A statement that follows logically from other facts.

cone: A solid figure with a circle as its base and a curved surface that meets at a point.

cones

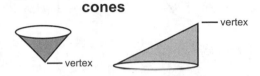

congruent figures: Figures that have the same shape and size.

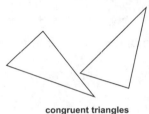

congruent triangles

coordinate grid or plane: A two-dimensional arrangement of parallel and evenly-spaced horizontal and vertical lines that is designed for locating points or displaying data.

coordinates: Ordered pairs of numbers that identify the location of points on a coordinate plane. Example: (3, 4) is the coordinate of point A.

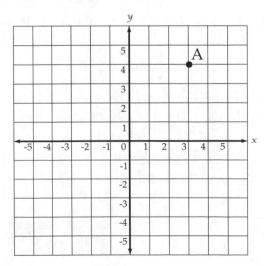

Glossary

cube: A solid figure with six faces that are congruent (equal) squares.

cylinder: A solid figure with two circular bases that are congruent (equal) and parallel to each other connected by a curved lateral surface.

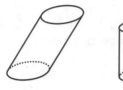

data: Information that is collected.

decimal number: A number written with a decimal point that is expressed in base 10, such as 39,456 where each digit's value is determined by multiplying it by some power of ten.

denominator: The bottom number in a fraction.

diagram: A drawing that represents a mathematical situation.

diameter: A line segment (or length of a segment) passing through the center of the circle with end points on the circle.

difference: The answer when subtracting two numbers.

direct measure: Obtaining the measure of an object by using a measuring device, such as a ruler, yardstick, meter stick, tape measure, scale, thermometer, measuring cup, or some other tool. Nonstandard devices, such as a paper clip or pencil may also be used.

distance: The length between two points.

dividend: A number in a division problem that is divided. Dividend ÷ divisor = quotient. Example: In 15 ÷ 3 = 5, 15 is the dividend.

$$\overset{\text{quotient}}{\text{divisor}\overline{)\text{dividend}}} \qquad 3\overline{)15}^{\,5}$$

divisible: A number that can be divided by another number without leaving a remainder. Example: 12 is divisible by 3 because 12 ÷ 3 is an integer, namely 4.

division: An operation that tells how many equal groups there are or how many are in each group.

divisor: The number by which another number is divided. Example: In 15 ÷ 3 = 5, 3 is the divisor.

$$\overset{\text{quotient}}{\text{divisor}\overline{)\text{dividend}}} \qquad 3\overline{)15}^{\,5}$$

edge: The line segment where two faces of a solid figure meet.

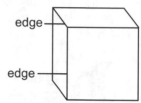

equality: Two or more sets of values that are equal.

equation: A number sentence that says two expressions are equal (=). Example: 4 + 8 = 6 + 6.

equivalent forms of a number: The same number expressed in different forms (e.g., $\frac{3}{4}$, 0.75, 75%).

equivalent fractions: Two fractions with equal values.

estimate: To find an approximate value or measurement of something without exact calculation.

evaluate an algebraic expression: Substitute numbers for the variables in the expression, then follow the algebraic order of operations to find the numerical value of the expression.

even number: A whole number that has a 0, 2, 4, 6, or 8 in the ones place. A number that is a multiple of 2. Examples: 0, 4, and 678 are even numbers.

expanded form: A number written as the sum of the values of its digits. Example: 546 = 500 + 40 + 6.

expression: A combination of variables, numbers, and symbols that represents a mathematical relationship.

extraneous information: Information not needed to solve the problem.

Glossary

face: One side of a three-dimensional figure. For example, a cube has six faces that are all squares. The pyramid below has five faces—four triangles and one square.

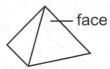

factor: One of two or more numbers that are multiplied together to give a product. Example: In 4 x 3 = 12, 4 and 3 are factors of 12.

fact family: A group of related facts using the same numbers. Example: 5 + 8 = 13; 13 − 8 = 5.

figure: A geometric figure is a set of points and/or lines in 2 or 3 dimensions.

flip (reflection): The change in a position of a figure that is the result of picking it up and turning it over. Example: Reversing a "b" to a "d." Tipping a "p" to a "b" or a "b" to a "p" as shown below:

fraction: A symbol, such as $\frac{2}{8}$ or $\frac{5}{3}$, used to name a part of a whole, a part of a set, or a location on the number line. Examples:

$$\frac{\text{numerator}}{\text{denominator}} = \frac{\text{dividend}}{\text{divisor}} =$$

$$\frac{\text{\# of parts under consideration}}{\text{\# of parts in a set}}$$

function: A relationship, such as a graph, in which a variable, called the dependent variable, is dependent on another value, usually an independent variable. In a function, each value of *x* corresponds to only one value of *y*.

function machine: Applies a function rule to a set of numbers, which determines a corresponding set of numbers. Example: Input 9 → Rule x 7 → Output 63. If you apply the function rule "multiply by 7" to the values 5, 7, and 9, the corresponding values are:

$$5 → 35$$
$$7 → 49$$
$$9 → 63$$

graph: A picture showing how certain facts are related to each other or how they compare to one another. Some examples of types of graphs are line graphs, pie charts, bar graphs, scatterplots, and pictographs.

grid: A pattern of regularly spaced horizontal and vertical lines on a plane that can be used to locate points and graph equations.

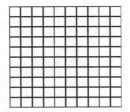

height: A line segment drawn from any vertex of a polygon to any side so that the line is perpendicular to the side to which it is drawn.

hexagon: A six-sided polygon. The total measure of the angles within a hexagon is 720°.

regular hexagon   irregular hexagons

impossible event: An event that can never happen.

indirect measure: To obtain data about an object by measuring another object or doing some calculation that allows you to infer what the actual measurement must be.

inequality: Two or more sets of values are not equal. There are a number of specific inequality types, including less than (<), greater than (>), and not equal to (≠).

Glossary

integer: Any number, positive or negative, that is a whole number distance away from zero on a number line, in addition to zero. Specifically, an integer is any number in the set {. . .-3,-2,-1, 0, 1, 2, 3. . .}. Examples of integers include 1, 5, 273, -2, -35, and -1,375.

intersecting lines: Lines that cross at a point. Examples:

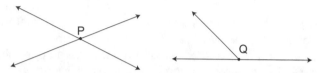

inverse operation: An action that undergoes a previously applied action. For example, subtraction is the inverse operation of addition.

isosceles triangle: A triangle with at least two sides that are the same length.

justify: To prove or show to be true or valid using logic and/or evidence.

key: An explanation of what each symbol represents in a pictograph.

kilometer (km): A metric unit of length. 1 kilometer = 1,000 meters.

labels (for a graph): The titles given to a graph, the axes of a graph, or to the scales on the axes of a graph.

length: A one-dimensional measure that is the measurable property of line segments.

likelihood: The chance that something is likely to happen.

line: A straight path of points that goes on forever in both directions.

line graph: A graph that uses a line or a curve to show how data changes over time.

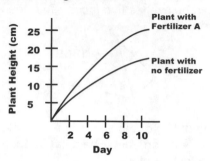

line of symmetry: A line on which a figure can be folded into two parts so that the parts match exactly.

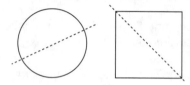

line segment: A part of a line with a beginning and an end point.

liter (L): A metric unit of capacity. 1 liter = 1,000 milliliters.

mass: The amount of matter in an object.

mean: Also called arithmetic average. A number found by adding two or more quantities together, and then dividing the sum by the number of quantities. For example, in the set {9, 5, 4} the mean is 6: 9 + 5 + 4 = 18; 18 ÷ 3 = 6. *See average.*

median: The middle number when numbers are put in order from least to greatest or from greatest to least. For example, in the set of numbers 6, 7, 8, 9, 10, the number 8 is the median (middle) number.

meter (m): A metric unit of length. 1 meter = 100 centimeters.

method: A systematic way of accomplishing a task.

mixed number: A number consisting of a whole number and a fraction. Example: $6\frac{2}{3}$.

Glossary

mode: The number or numbers that occur most often in a set of data. Example: The mode of {1, 3, 4, 5, 5, 7, 9} is 5.

multiple: A product of a number and any other whole number. Examples: {2, 4, 6, 8, 10, 12, …} are multiples of 2.

multiplication: An operation on two numbers that tells how many in all. The first number is the number of sets and the second number tells how many in each set.

natural numbers (counting numbers): The set of positive integers used for counting {1, 2, 3, 4, 5, …}.

nonstandard units of measure: Objects, such as blocks, paper clips or pencils that can be used to measure objects.

number line: A line that shows numbers in order using a scale. Equal intervals are marked and usually labeled on the number line.

number sentence: An expression of a relationship between quantities as an equation or an inequality. Examples: 7 + 7 = 8 + 6; 14 < 92; 56 + 4 > 59.

numerator: The top number in a fraction.

obtuse angle: An angle with a measure greater than 90 degrees and less than 180 degrees.

octagon: An eight-sided polygon. The total measure of the angles within an octagon is 1,080°.

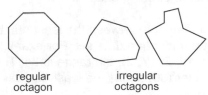

regular   irregular
octagon   octagons

odd number: A whole number that has 1, 3, 5, 7, or 9 in the ones place. An odd number is not divisible by 2. Examples: The numbers 53 and 701 are odd numbers.

operation: A mathematical process that combines numbers; basic operations of arithmetic include addition, subtraction, multiplication, and division.

order: To arrange numbers from the least to greatest or from the greatest to least.

ordered pair: Two numbers inside a set of parentheses separated by a comma that are used to name a point on a coordinate grid. Example: (2, 5).

organized data: Data arranged in a way that is meaningful and that assists in the interpretation of that data.

parallelogram: A quadrilateral in which opposite sides are parallel.

parallel lines: Lines in the same plane that never intersect.

pattern: An arrangement of numbers, pictures, etc., in an organized and predictable way. Examples: 3, 6, 9, 12 or ® 0 ® 0 ® 0.

pentagon: A five-sided polygon. The total measure of the angles within a pentagon is 540°.

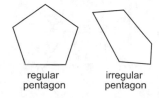

regular   irregular
pentagon   pentagon

percent: A ratio of a number to 100. Percent means per hundred and is represented by the symbol %. Example: "35 to 100" means 35%.

perimeter: The distance around a figure.

perpendicular lines: Two lines that intersect to form a right angle (90 degrees).

90°

pictograph: A graph that uses pictures or symbols to represent similar data. The value of each picture is interpreted by a "key" or "legend."

Key
Each picture =
10 pieces of fruit

Glossary

place value: The value given to the place a digit has in a number. Example: In the number 135, the 1 is in the hundreds place so it represents 100 (1 x 100), the 3 is in the tens place so it represents 30 (3 x 10), and the 5 is in the ones place so it represents 5 (5 x 1).

plane: Any region that can be defined by a minimum of three noncollinear points and that extends infinitely in a two-dimensional manner. It's like an infinite piece of paper with no thickness.

plane figure: An arrangement of points, lines, or curves within a single plane: a "flat" figure.

P.M.: The hours from noon to midnight; from the Latin words *post meridiem* meaning after noon.

point: An exact position often marked by a dot.

polygon: A closed figure made up of straight line segments.

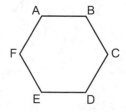

ABCDEF is a polygon.

possible event: An event that might or might not happen.

predict: To tell what you believe may happen in the future.

prediction: A prediction is a description of what may happen before it happens.

prime number: A whole number greater than 1 having exactly two whole number factors, itself, and 1. Examples: The number 7 is prime since its only whole number factors are 1 and 7. One is not a prime number.

probability: The likelihood that something will happen.

product: The answer to a multiplication problem. Example: In 3 x 4 = 12, 12 is the product.

pyramid: A solid figure in which the base is a polygon and whose faces are triangles with a common point called a vertex.

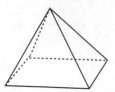

quadrilateral: A four-sided polygon. Rectangles, squares, parallelograms, rhombi, and trapezoids are all quadrilaterals. The total measure of the angles within a quadrilateral is 360°. Example: ABCD is a quadrilateral.

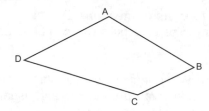

questionnaire: A set of questions for a survey.

quotient: The answer in a division problem. Dividend ÷ divisor = quotient. Example: In 15 ÷ 3 = 5, 5 is the quotient.

radius: The distance from the center to the edge of a circle; or, the distance from the center of a circle to a point on the circle.

randomly (chosen): When all items within a set have an equal chance of being chosen.

range: The difference between the least number and the greatest number in a data set. For example, in the set {4, 7, 10, 12, 36, 7, 2}, the range is 34. The greatest number (36) minus the least number (2): (36 − 2 = 34).

ratio: A comparison of two numbers using a variety of written forms. Example: The ratio of two and five may be written "2 to 5" or 2:5 or 2/5.

ray: A straight line extending infinitely in one direction from a given point.

Copying is Prohibited © Englefield & Associates, Inc.

Glossary

rectangle: A quadrilateral with four right angles. A square is one example of a rectangle.

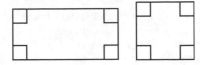

reflection: The change in the position of a figure that is the result of picking it up and turning it over. *See flip.*

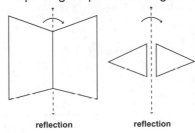

reflection   reflection

regular polygon: A special type of polygon that is both equilateral and equiangular.

relative size: The size of one number in comparison to another number or numbers.

represent: To present clearly; describe; show.

remainder: The number that is left over after dividing. Example: In 31 ÷ 7 = 4 R 3, the 3 is the remainder.

rhombus: A quadrilateral with opposite sides parallel and all sides the same length. A square is one kind of rhombus.

right angle: An angle that forms a square corner and measures 90 degrees.

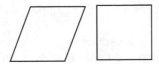

right prism or rectangular solid: A three-dimensional figure (polyhedron) with congruent, polygonal or rectangular bases, and lateral faces that are all rectangles.

right triangle: A triangle having one right angle. *See angle and triangle.*

rotation: Moving an object around an imaginary point in a circular motion either clockwise or counterclockwise. After the move, the object will have the same shape and size but may be facing a different direction. *See turn.*

rounding: Replacing a number with a number that tells about how much or how many to the nearest ten, hundred, thousand, and so on. Example: 52 rounded to the nearest 10 is 50.

rule: A procedure; a prescribed method; a way of describing the relationship between two sets of numbers. Example: In the following data, the rule is to add 3:

Input	Output
3	6
5	8
9	12

ruler: A straight-edged instrument used for measuring the lengths of objects. A ruler usually measures smaller units of length, such as inches or centimeters.

scale: The numbers that show the units used on a graph.

scale model: A model or drawing based on a ratio of the dimensions for the model and the actual object it represents.

sequence: A set of numbers arranged in a special order or pattern.

set: A group made up of numbers, figures, or parts.

side: A line segment connected to other segments to form the boundary of a polygon.

←side

similar: A description for figures that are the same shape, but might not be the same size or in the same position.

slide (translation): The change in the position of a figure that moves up, down, or sideways. Example: scooting a book on a table.

Glossary

solids: Figures in three dimensions.

solve: To find the solution to an equation or problem; finding the values of unknown variables that will make a true mathematical statement.

sphere: A solid figure in the shape of a ball. Example: a basketball is a sphere.

square: A rectangle with congruent (equal) sides. *See rectangle.*

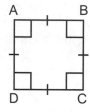

square number: The product of a number multiplied by itself. Example: 49 is a square number (7 x 7 = 49).

square unit: The square with sides 1 unit long used to measure area.

squiggle: *See break.*

standard form: A way to write a number showing only its digits. Example: 2,389.

standard units of measure: Units of measure commonly used; generally classified in the U.S. as the customary system or the metric system:

```
Customary System:
    Length
    1 foot (ft) = 12 inches (in)
    1 yard (yd) = 3 feet or 36 inches
    1 mile (mi) = 1,760 yards or 5,280 feet

    Weight
    16 ounces (oz) = 1 pound (lb)
    2,000 pounds = 1 ton (t)

    Capacity
    1 pint (pt) = 2 cups (c)
    1 quart (qt) = 2 pints
    1 gallon (gal) = 4 quarts

    Temperature
    degrees Fahrenheit (°F)
```

```
Metric System:
    Length
    1 centimeter (cm) = 10 millimeters (mm)
    1 decimeter (dm) = 10 centimeters
    1 meter (m) = 100 centimeters
    1 kilometer (km) = 1,000 meters

    Weight
    1,000 milligrams (mg) = 1 gram (g)
    1,000 grams (g) = 1 kilogram (kg)

    Capacity
    1 liter (l)  = 1,000 milliliters (ml)

    Temperature
    degrees Celsius (°C)
```

stem-and-leaf plot: A type of graph that depicts data by occurrence using commonalities in place value. The digit in the tens place is used as the stem. The digit in the ones place is used as the leaf.

straight angle: An angle with a measure of 180°; this is also a straight line.

strategy: A plan used in problem solving, such as looking for a pattern, drawing a diagram, working backward, etc.

subtraction: The operation that finds the difference between two numbers.

sum: The answer when adding two or more addends: addend + addend = sum.

summary: A series of statements containing evidence, facts, and/or procedures that support a result.

survey: A way to collect data by asking a certain number of people the same question and recording their answers.

symmetry: A figure has symmetry if it can be folded along a line so that both parts match exactly.

table: A method of displaying data about a topic into rows and columns.

Glossary

temperature: A measure of hot or cold in degrees.

transformation: An operation on a geometric figure by which another image is created. Common transformations include reflections (flips), translations (slides), rotations (turns), dilations, and contractions.

translation: A change in the position of a figure that moves it up, down, or sideways. *See slide.*

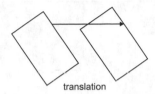

translation

tree diagram: A visual diagram of all the possible outcomes for a certain event. A tree diagram is used to show the probability of a certain event happening.

trend line: A line on a graph that indicates a statistical trend, or tendency of a set of data to move in a certain direction.

triangle: A polygon with three sides. The sum of the angles of a triangle is always equal to 180°.

turn (rotation): The change in the position of a figure that moves it around a point. Example: The hands of a clock turn around the center of the clock in a clockwise direction.

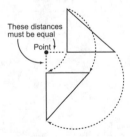

These distances must be equal

Point

unlikely event: An event that probably will not happen.

unorganized data: Randomly presented data that is not presented in a meaningful way.

variable: A symbol used to represent a quantity that is unknown, that changes, or that can have different values. Example: in 5n, the *n* is a variable.

vertex: The point where two rays meet to form an angle or where the sides of a polygon meet or the point where 3 or more edges meet in a solid figure.

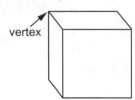

vertex

vertices: The plural of vertex.

volume: The amount of area taken up by a three-dimensional object. The units of measurement used to express volume can be cubic units, such as cubic feet or cubic centimeters, or when measuring fluids, units such as gallons or liters. Volume is usually abbreviated as *V* and is also called capacity.

weight: A measurement of the amount of force by gravity on a object.

whole number: An integer in the set {0, 1, 2, 3 . . .}. In other words, a whole number is any number used when counting in addition to zero.

word forms: The number written in words. Examples: 546 is "five hundred forty-six." The "<" symbol means "is less than." The ">" symbol means "is greater than." The "=" symbol means "equals" or "is equal to."

***x*-axis:** One of two intersecting straight (number) lines that determine a coordinate system in a plane; typically the horizontal axis.

***y*-axis:** One of two intersecting straight (number) lines that determine a coordinate system in a plane; typically the vertical axis.

Examples of Common Two-Dimensional Shapes

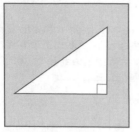
Right Triangle

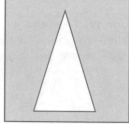
Isosceles Triangle

Equilateral Triangle

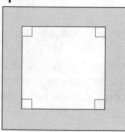
Square

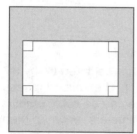
Rectangle

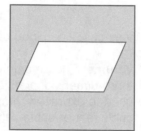
Parallelogram

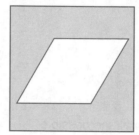
Rhombus

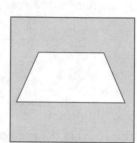
Trapezoid

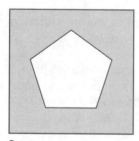
Pentagon

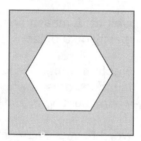
Hexagon

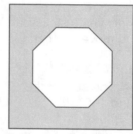
Octagon

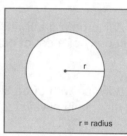
Circle

Examples of Common Three-Dimensional Shapes

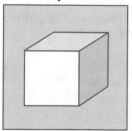
Cube

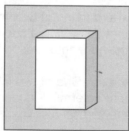
Rectangular Prism

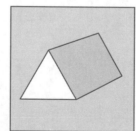
Triangular Prism

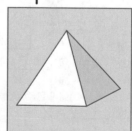
Pyramid

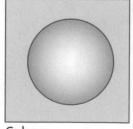
Sphere

Cylinder

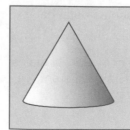
Cone

Examples of How Lines Interact

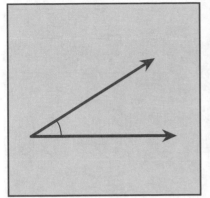

Acute Angle

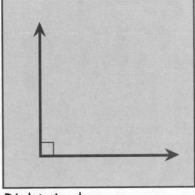

Right Angle

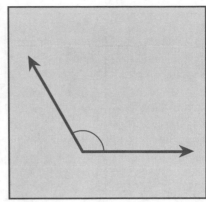

Obtuse Angle

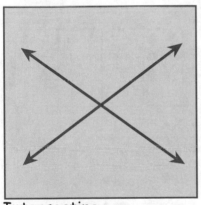

Intersecting

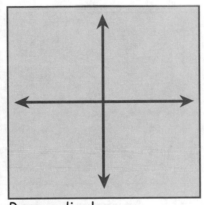

Perpendicular

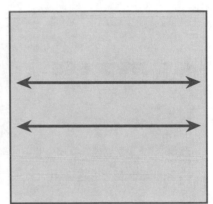

Parallel

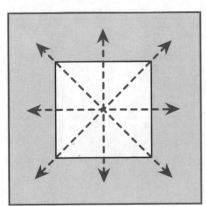

Lines of Symmetry

Examples of Types of Graphs

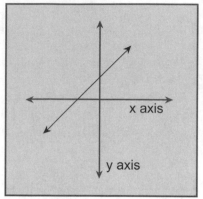

Line Graph

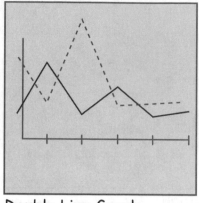

Double Line Graph

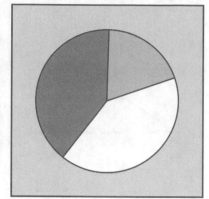

Pie Chart

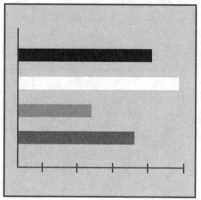

Bar Graph

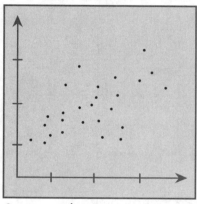

Scatterplot

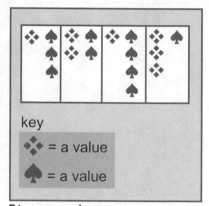

Pictograph

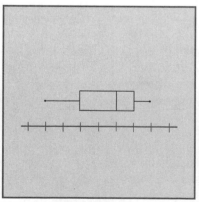

Stem and Leaf Plot

Box and Whisker

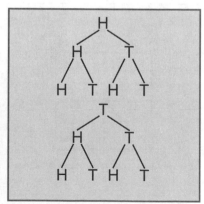

Tree Diagram

Examples of Object Movement

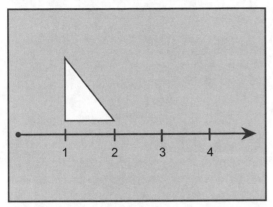
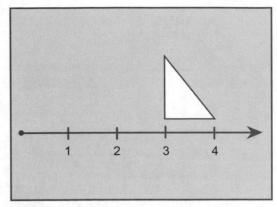

Translation

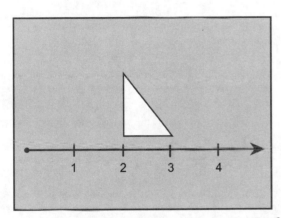
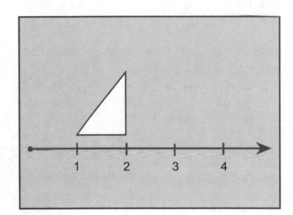

Reflection

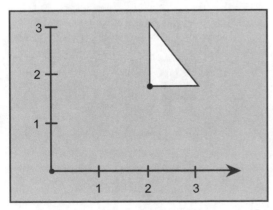
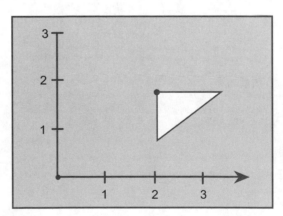

Rotation

BLANK PAGE

Mathematics Practice Tutorial

Directions for Taking the Mathematics Practice Tutorial

The Mathematics Practice Tutorial contains 33 practice questions. You will mark your answers in this book. If you don't understand a question, just ask your teacher to explain it to you. Calculators and rulers are NOT to be used on the Mathematics Practice Tutorial.

This section will review the Strands, Standards, and Benchmarks used to assess student achievement in the state of Florida. Following the description of each Benchmark, a sample mathematics practice item is given. Each item gives you an idea of how the Benchmark may be assessed. Review these items to increase your familiarity with FCAT-style multiple-choice, gridded-response, and short- and extended-response items. Once you have read through this Tutorial section, you will be ready to complete the full-length Mathematics Assessment.

Sample Multiple-Choice Item

To help you understand how to answer the test questions, look at the sample test question below. It is included to show you what a multiple-choice item in the test is like and how to mark your answer.

1 Aaron and Michelle need to collect 52 leaves for their science project. They have 18 leaves so far. Which operation should be used in the box below to find how many more leaves they need?

$$52 \;\boxed{?}\; 18 =$$

Ⓐ addition

Ⓑ division

Ⓒ multiplication

● subtraction

For this sample question, the correct choice is Answer D "subtraction"; therefore, the circle next to Answer D is filled in.

Sample Gridded-Response Item

To help you understand how to answer the test questions, look at the sample test question below. It is included to show you what a gridded-response item in the test is like and how to mark your answer.

 Mathematics test questions with this symbol require that you fill in a grid in this workbook. There may be more than one correct way to fill in a response grid. The gridded-response section on page 103 will show you the different ways the response grid may be completed.

2 Ashley, Doug, Penny, and Susan had a contest to see who could sell the most lollipops. The graph below shows the number of lollipops each of them sold.

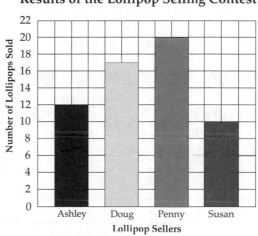

How many lollipops, all together, were sold?

For this sample question, the correct answer is 59 lollipops. The number 5 is written in the tens place on the grid, and number 9 is written in the ones place. The circles underneath the written 5 and written 9 are filled in.

Go On ▶

Sample Short-Response Item

To help you understand how to answer the test questions, look at the sample test question below. It is included to show you what a short-response item in the test is like and how to write your answer.

 Mathematics test questions with this symbol require that you answer a short-response item. For this type of question, you will write an answer using words, numbers, or pictures. Each short-response item receives a single score of 0, 1, or 2 points.

---

3 Park Elementary School's fifth graders were collecting cans for recycling. On Friday they collected 12.35 pounds of cans, on Saturday they collected 21.7 pounds of cans, and on Sunday they collected 35.65 pounds of cans. ESTIMATE how many pounds of cans they collected in these three days and explain your answer.

Estimated pounds of cans: <u>70</u>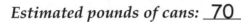

<u>Round off each weight to the nearest whole pound and then add</u>

<u>the rounded amounts: 12.35 ≈ 12, 21.7 ≈ 22, and 35.65 ≈ 36;</u>

<u>12 + 22 + 36 = 70.</u>

Sample Extended-Response Item

To help you understand how to answer the test questions, look at the sample test question below. It is included to show you what an extended-response item in the test is like and how to write your answer.

Mathematics test questions with this symbol require that you answer an extended-response item. For this type of question, you will write an answer using words, numbers, or pictures. Each extended-response item receives a single score of 0, 1, 2, 3, or 4 points.

4 Sales data for two bookstores is shown on these pictographs.

The Book Nook Bookstore	
Kind of Book	
Mystery	📘📘📘📘
Science Fiction	📘📘📘📘📘📘
Humor	📘📘📘📘

 = 2 books

Sir Read-A-Lot Bookstore	
Kind of Book	
Mystery	📘📘📘
Science Fiction	📘📘📘
Humor	📘📘📘📘

📘 = 5 books

Part A

Which bookstore sold more science fiction books? __Sir Read-A-Lot Bookstore__

Explain your answer on the lines below.

Sir Read-A-Lot sold more science fiction books. Each symbol on the Sir Read-A-Lot pictograph stands for 5 books. There are 3 symbols shown for science fiction, so 15 (3 x 5 = 15) science fiction books were sold. Each symbol on the Book Nook pictograph stands for 2 books. There are 6 symbols shown for science fiction, so 12 (2 x 6 = 12) science fiction books were sold.

Part B

Which bookstore sold the most mystery books? <u>Sir Read-A-Lot Bookstore</u>

Explain your answer on the lines below.

<u>Sir Read-A-Lot sold more mystery books. Each symbol on the Sir</u>

<u>Read-A-Lot pictograph stands for 5 books. There are 4 symbols</u>

<u>shown for mystery, so 20 (4 x 5 = 20) mystery books were sold.</u>

<u>Each symbol on the Book Nook pictograph stands for 2 books.</u>

<u>There are 4 symbols shown for mystery, so 8 (2 x 4 = 8) mystery</u>

<u>books were sold.</u>

<u>   </u>

Mathematics Practice Tutorial

1 What number is in the hundreds place in the number **74,032**?

    Ⓐ 0

    Ⓑ 3

    Ⓒ 4

    Ⓓ 7

2 Which of the answer choices lists the following numbers from **least** to **greatest**?

$$\frac{47}{100};\ 0.43;\ \frac{40}{100};\ 0.50$$

    Ⓕ $0.43;\ \frac{47}{100};\ \frac{40}{100};\ 0.50$

    Ⓖ $\frac{40}{100};\ \frac{47}{100};\ 0.43;\ 0.50$

    Ⓗ $0.50;\ \frac{47}{100};\ 0.43;\ \frac{40}{100}$

    Ⓘ $\frac{40}{100};\ 0.43;\ \frac{47}{100};\ 0.50$

Go On ▶

3 Which picture below shows 75% of the pizza has been eaten?

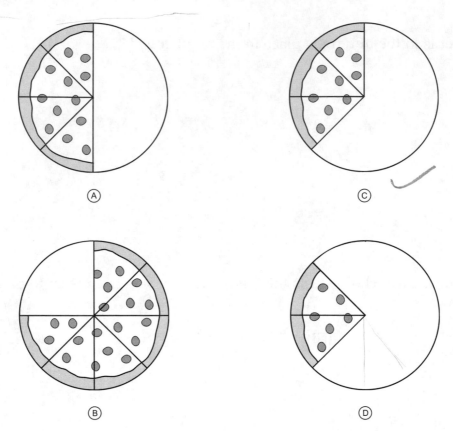

Ⓐ

Ⓒ

Ⓑ

Ⓓ

4 Which of the following is NOT another way of writing 50%?

ⓕ $\frac{1}{2}$

ⓖ 0.50

ⓗ 0.05

ⓘ $\frac{5}{10}$

5 Mr. Barliman gives his math class an extra-credit assignment every week. This week, Mr. Barliman gives his class a mystery number to find. Use the clues given below to determine Mr. Barliman's mystery number.

I am the largest 3-digit number containing the numbers 3, 7, and 8 that is also a multiple of 2. What number am I?

6 In the expression below, which operations will result in the same answer?

$$7 \boxed{?} 1$$

Ⓐ addition and multiplication

Ⓑ division and multiplication

Ⓒ subtraction and division

Ⓓ subtraction and addition

7 Jethro's father's age is 5 less than 4 times Jethro's age. If Jethro is 10 years old, which expression below represents how old Jethro's father is?

Ⓕ $(10 \times 5) - 4$

Ⓖ $(10 \times 4) - 5$

Ⓗ $(10 \times 4) + 5$

Ⓘ $(10 \times 5) + 4$

8 Patty was selling cookies in her neighborhood for a school fundraiser. On the first street, she was able to sell 9 boxes of cookies. On the next street, Patty sold 3 times as many boxes of cookies. What is the total number of boxes of cookies Patty sold?

Ⓐ 12 boxes of cookies

Ⓑ 18 boxes of cookies

Ⓒ 27 boxes of cookies

Ⓓ 36 boxes of cookies

Copying is Prohibited © Englefield & Associates, Inc.

9 THINK SOLVE EXPLAIN

Emilio and his friends are doing a puzzle. The part of the puzzle they have completed is shown below.

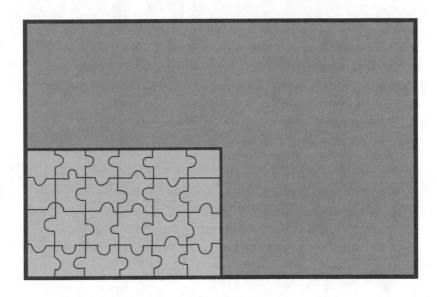

Using the picture, ESTIMATE the total number of pieces the finished puzzle will have and explain your answer on the lines below.

_____

_____

_____

_____

_____

_____

10 Gerard is packing away some clothes that do not fit him any longer. He has 36 sweaters to put in boxes. If he is going to divide the sweaters evenly. What is the **greatest** number of sweaters he might have in one box?

F 4 sweaters

G 9 sweaters

H 13 sweaters

I 16 sweaters

11 Jennifer is helping her dad put new shingles on the roof of their house. They know it will take 4,672 shingles to cover the entire roof. Each shingle is the same size as the shingle pictured below.

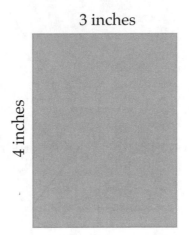

3 inches

4 inches

Part A
Explain how Jennifer and her dad can determine how much total area the shingles will cover.

_____

_____

_____

_____

_____

Part B
Find out how much total area the shingles will cover. (Area = length x width)

_____

_____

_____

12 Mr. Duncan put a stone fence around his garden, which is shown below.

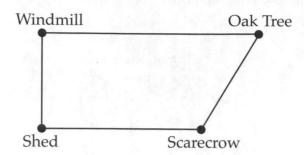

What object is located at the point in the fence where the angle formed by the fence is obtuse?

- Ⓐ Windmill
- Ⓑ Oak Tree
- Ⓒ Scarecrow
- Ⓓ Shed

13 The Liberty Bell weighs about 2,080 pounds. How much does the Liberty Bell weigh in ounces? (1 pound = 16 ounces)

- Ⓕ 130 ounces
- Ⓖ 1,300 ounces
- Ⓗ 3,380 ounces
- Ⓘ 33,280 ounces

14 Which of the following **most likely** describes the length of a paper clip?

Ⓐ 3 millimeters

Ⓑ 3 centimeters

Ⓒ 3 meters

Ⓓ 3 kilometers

15 Dale wants to buy his friend Eloise flowers. Each bouquet of flowers costs $3.95. Dale wants to buy Eloise 5 bouquets of flowers.

THINK
SOLVE
EXPLAIN

ESTIMATE how much money Dale will need to take to the flower shop. Explain how you made your estimate and if it is a good estimate or not. (Do not worry about sales tax.)

_____

_____

_____

_____

_____

_____

_____

16 The workers at the local zoo are preparing a new tank for the sea lion exhibit. They are trying to calculate how much water they will need to fill the tank. What unit of measurement will they use to describe the amount of water the new tank will hold?

Ⓕ gallons

Ⓖ tons

Ⓗ square feet

Ⓘ degrees

17 Which measuring device would be **best** to weigh vegetables at the grocery store?

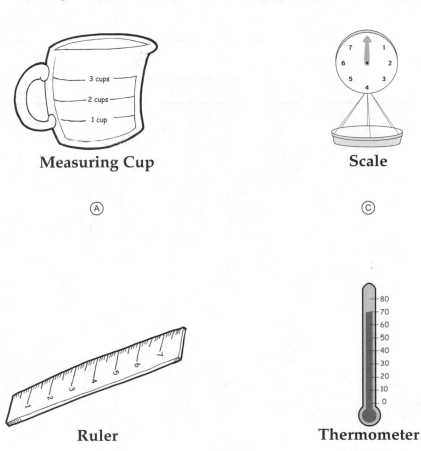

Measuring Cup

Ⓐ

Scale

Ⓒ

Ruler

Ⓑ

Thermometer

Ⓓ

18 THINK SOLVE EXPLAIN

Give a description of the shape below. Include at least three characteristics of the figure in your description.

_____

_____

_____

_____

19 Which shape has the **most** lines of symmetry?

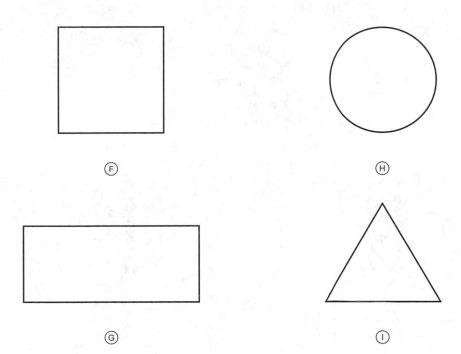

F

H

G

I

Go On ▶

20 Harvey rotated the ladybug picture 180°. Then, he flipped it around an imaginary vertical line. Finally, he rotated the picture another 180°. What did the picture look like after the second rotation?

Ⓐ

Ⓒ

Ⓑ

Ⓓ

Go On ▶

Copying is Prohibited

© Englefield & Associates, Inc.

21 What coordinates will make a figure with two pairs of congruent sides when plotted with the points on the graph below?

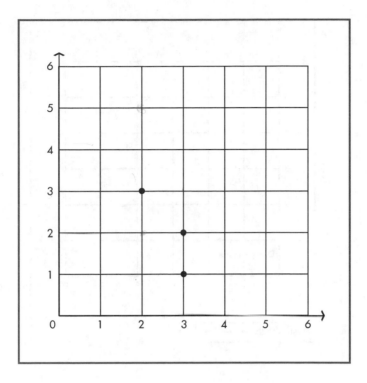

Ⓕ (2, 5)

Ⓖ (1, 4)

Ⓗ (2, 2)

Ⓘ (3, 2)

Go On ▶

22 The grid below shows the path Dusty takes to get from his house to school. Which coordinates does Dusty's path cross?

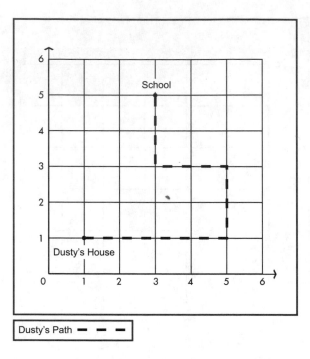

Dusty's Path — — —

Ⓐ (1, 5)

Ⓑ (4, 1)

Ⓒ (3, 2)

Ⓓ (3, 6)

23 What is the missing number in the pattern listed below?

4, 8, 12, 24, 36, 56, 60

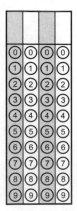

24 Julie and her friends had a lemonade stand in their neighborhood. They noticed that as the temperature went up, they sold more cups of lemonade. They made the table shown below to show this pattern.

Lemonade Stand Selling Pattern					
Temperature	80° F	82° F	84° F	86° F	88° F
Cups Sold	12	19	26	33	

Part A
Use the pattern to determine how many cups of lemonade they will sell when the temperature is 88° F.

_____

_____

_____

Part B
Explain how the change in temperature affects the number of cups of lemonade sold.

_____

_____

_____

_____

_____

_____

25 Howard is 5 years younger than his older sister Kathryn. If *h* represents Howard's age, which expression could be used to find Kathryn's age?

    Ⓕ $h \times 5$

    Ⓖ $h \div 5$

    Ⓗ $h - 5$

    Ⓘ $h + 5$

26 Carmen plays on her school's basketball team. In the first game of the season, she only played for 8 minutes of the game. During the team's next game, she played 5 minutes more than twice the number of minutes she had played in the team's first game. How many total minutes did she play in the first two games of the season?

    Ⓐ 13 minutes

    Ⓑ 21 minutes

    Ⓒ 26 minutes

    Ⓓ 29 minutes

27 Each fifth grader at Reagan Elementary School voted for his or her favorite field day event. The results of the vote are shown in the bar graph below.

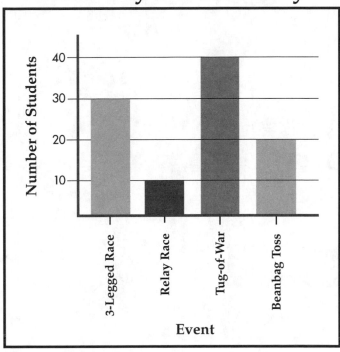

How many fifth graders attend Reagan Elementary School?

28 Genevieve was competing in a fishing contest. She caught 7 fish during the competition. The smallest fish she caught weighed 5 pounds. The heaviest fish she caught weighed 9 pounds. Which weight could have been the **median** weight of the 7 fish Genevieve caught?

     Ⓕ 3 pounds

     Ⓖ 4 pounds

     Ⓗ 7 pounds

     Ⓘ 14 pounds

29 The scores Bernardo received on the 7 spelling tests in Mrs. Verbosky's class are shown in the graph below.

THINK
SOLVE
EXPLAIN

Bernardo's Spelling Test Scores

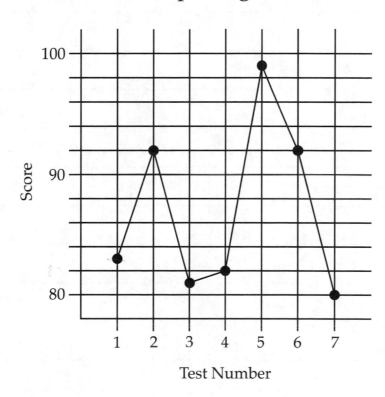

Part A

Determine the **mean**, **median**, **mode**, and **range** of the data.

_____

_____

_____

_____

_____

_____

_____

_____

_____

_____

_____

_____

_____

_____

_____

_____

_____

_____

Part B

Determine which one of those values best represents Bernardo's overall performance on the tests. Explain your choice.

_____

_____

_____

_____

_____

_____

_____

30 Jacques has forgotten his locker combination. He knows that the 3 numbers in the combination are 19, 25, and 27. What are all the possible combinations Jacques could try to open his locker?

THINK
SOLVE
EXPLAIN

_____

_____

_____

_____

_____

Copying is Prohibited   © Englefield & Associates, Inc.

31 Mr. Ferguson told his American history class what types of questions to expect on their next test. He said there would be 50 questions total. Of those questions, 25 would be multiple-choice questions, 15 would be matching questions, and the rest would be fill-in-the-blank questions. What is the probability that the first question on the test is a multiple-choice question?

Ⓐ $\frac{1}{5}$

Ⓑ $\frac{1}{4}$

Ⓒ $\frac{1}{2}$

Ⓓ $\frac{2}{5}$

32 Julio's school is going to buy a new piece of playground equipment. Since he is the student council president, Julio is asked by the principal to find out the opinions of the students. Which method should Julio use to find the opinions of the other students in the school?

Ⓕ Julio should take a survey of students who stay in the library during recess.

Ⓖ Julio should take a survey of students at a local park.

Ⓗ Julio should take a survey of students as they enter the cafeteria for lunch.

Ⓘ Julio should take a survey of students who use the swings at recess.

33 The table below shows the batting average of the American League batting champion for 5 years.

Name	Average	Year
Frank Thomas	0.347	1997
Bernie Williams	0.339	1998
Nomar Garciaparra	0.357	1999
Nomar Garciaparra	0.372	2000
Ichiro Suzuki	0.350	2001

Using the data given, predict what the American League batting champion's batting average will be for 2002. Explain your prediction.

_____

_____

_____

_____

_____

_____

This is the end of the Mathematics Practice Tutorial.
Until time is called, go back and check your work or answer questions you did
not complete. When you have finished, close your workbook.

Mathematics Assessment

Directions for Taking the Mathematics Assessment Test

This Assessment contains 50–55 questions. For multiple-choice questions, you will be asked to pick the best answer out of four possible choices. Fill in the answer bubble to mark your selection. On gridded-response questions, each question requires a numerical answer which should be filled into a four-column number grid. You will also be asked short-response and extended-response questions, which may require you to complete more than one step and to explain your answer using words, numbers, and/or pictures.

Read each question carefully and answer it to the best of your ability. If you do not know an answer, you may skip the question and come back to it later.

Figures and diagrams with given lengths and/or dimensions are NOT drawn to scale. Angle measures should be assumed to be accurate. Any formulas or measurement conversions you need will be provided in the question.

When you finish, check your answers.

Mathematics Assessment

1 Jillian and her friend Indira were jumping rope together. Jillian was able to complete 11 jumps in a row more than the number of jumps Indira was able to jump in a row. If j represents the number of times Jillian was able to jump in a row, which expression could be used to find the number of times Indira could jump in a row?

    Ⓐ $j - 11$

    Ⓑ $j + 11$

    Ⓒ $j \times 11$

    Ⓓ $j \div 11$

---

2 Mrs. Busca's class was having a scavenger hunt on the playground. Each student needed to find a red pebble, a yellow leaf, and a stick shaped like a Y.

THINK
SOLVE
EXPLAIN

If the students were allowed to find these items in any order, what are all the possible orders in which students might find the three items?

You may use the first letters of the items to represent the items if you like (for example, p = pebble, l = leaf, and s = stick).

_____

_____

---

3 Which number is seven hundred six thousand thirty-nine?

    Ⓕ 700,600,039

    Ⓖ 7,006,039

    Ⓗ 706,039

    Ⓘ 706.039

4 The owner of Hero of the Day sub shop keeps track of the number of people who order the lunch special each day. The tables below show the number of people who bought the daily lunch special for each of the past 3 weeks. Monday's special is always pizza subs.

WEEK 1		
Day	**Special**	**Customers**
Monday	Pizza Sub	52
Tuesday	Tuna Melt	27
Wednesday	Italian	49
Thursday	BLT	33
Friday	Meatball	47

WEEK 2		
Day	**Special**	**Customers**
Monday	Pizza Sub	61
Tuesday	Tuna Melt	33
Wednesday	Italian	46
Thursday	BLT	41
Friday	Meatball	62

WEEK 3		
Day	**Special**	**Customers**
Monday	Pizza Sub	54
Tuesday	Tuna Melt	36
Wednesday	Italian	53
Thursday	BLT	35
Friday	Meatball	64

What is the **best** prediction of the total number of customers who will order the lunch special on Monday of Week 4?

Ⓐ 39 customers

Ⓑ 42 customers

Ⓒ 47 customers

Ⓓ 60 customers

5 Lucy cannot remember the password she chose to protect her email. She knows she chose a numerical password with four digits. The four digits in the password are 1, 6, 7, and 9.

If Lucy's password is the greatest four-digit number which can be formed using these four numbers, what is Lucy's password?

6 Flora planted tulips in her garden last fall. In the spring, only about 25% of the tulips she planted grew. The diagram below shows how many tulips grew in one area of Flora's garden. Flora planted tulips in all 8 of her flower beds.

THINK
SOLVE
EXPLAIN

Part A
Use the diagram below to ESTIMATE how many tulips Flora planted last fall.

_____

_____

Part B
Explain your estimate on the lines provided.

_____

_____

_____

_____

_____

_____

Go On ▶

7 Which pair of shapes is congruent?

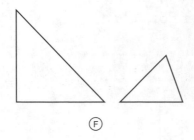

F

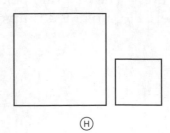

H

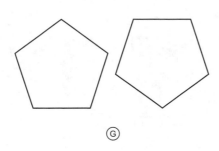

G

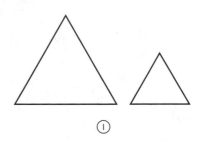

I

8 Kenya went to the circus with her family. She especially enjoyed watching the lions and tigers. While she was watching the lions and tigers jump through hoops, she noticed that each of the 7 lions was able to jump through 6 hoops at once, and each of the 6 tigers could jump through 5 hoops at once. Which expression could be used to find the total number of hoops all the lions and tigers jumped through?

- Ⓐ 7 + 5 x 6
- Ⓑ (7 x 6) + (6 x 5)
- Ⓒ (7 + 6) x (6 + 5)
- Ⓓ (7 + 6) x 6 x 5

Go On ▶

9 Juniper and her friends were doing a science project with Flubble Bubble Gum. They wanted to see what size bubble could be blown with a certain number of pieces of Flubble. The chart below shows their results. The bubble size in the chart is the biggest bubble that was blown using a certain number of pieces of Flubble.

Flubble Bubble Gum Experiment					
Pieces	1	2	3	4	5
Size	5 in.	6.5 in.	8 in.	9.5 in.	

Part A
Using the data given in the chart, determine the biggest bubble that could be blown with 5 pieces of Flubble.

_____

_____

_____

_____

Part B
Explain how the size of the bubble changes as the number of pieces of Flubble used changes.

_____

_____

_____

_____

10 A new flagpole is being installed at Patriot Elementary School. What unit of measurement would be **most** appropriate to measure how far around the flagpole is at its base?

  (F) milliliters

  (G) circles

  (H) miles

  (I) inches

11 Marisol and her friends decided to have a paper airplane contest. Each of them constructed a paper airplane to see how far it would fly. Their results are shown in the table below.

Name	Flight Length
Marisol	4.25 feet
Richard	3.90 feet
Bonnie	4.09 feet
Mario	4.209 feet

According to the table, which of the following lists the names of Marisol and her friends in order from the person with the **shortest** paper airplane flight to the person with the **longest** paper airplane flight?

  (A) Marisol, Mario, Bonnie, Richard

  (B) Richard, Marisol, Mario, Bonnie

  (C) Richard, Bonnie, Marisol, Mario

  (D) Richard, Bonnie, Mario, Marisol

12 An elephant runs at a speed of 25 miles per hour. If an elephant was able to travel at this speed for 6 hours, how far would the elephant have traveled at the end of the 6 hours?

⒡   31 miles

⒢   90 miles

⒣   125 miles

⒤   150 miles

13 Look at the pattern below. How many sides will the **eighth** figure in the pattern have?

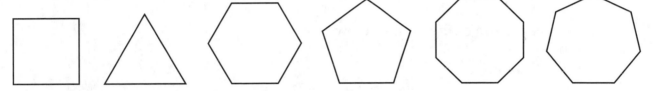

14 About 20% of Earth's atmosphere is oxygen. What fraction of Earth's atmosphere is oxygen?

- Ⓐ $\frac{1}{20}$

- Ⓑ $\frac{2}{5}$

- Ⓒ $\frac{20}{100}$

- Ⓓ $\frac{10}{20}$

15 Look at the picture of the whale below.

Which picture shows the whale after it has been rotated 180°?

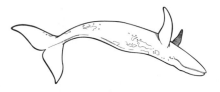

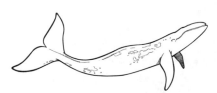

Ⓕ   Ⓗ

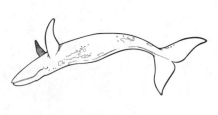

Ⓖ   Ⓘ

16 Federico's mother is putting wallpaper up in his room.

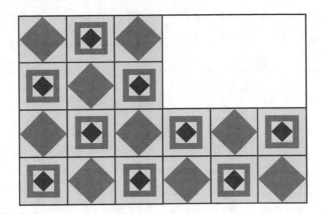

What percent of the wall shown above does NOT have wallpaper on it yet?

Ⓐ 25%

Ⓑ 50%

Ⓒ 66%

Ⓓ 75%

17 A cereal company ships boxes of cereal in cartons containing 20 boxes of cereal each carton. The boxes of cereal are arranged in two layers stacked top to bottom; each layer has 2 rows of 5 boxes. The top view of one of the layers is shown below, along with the measurements of the top of 1 box of cereal.

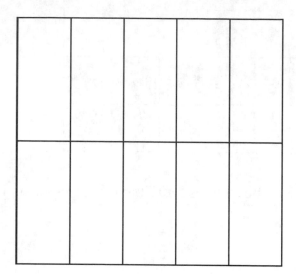

3 inches

8 inches

What is the **perimeter** of the top of one layer of cereal boxes?

   Ⓕ   220 inches

   Ⓖ   110 inches

   Ⓗ   62 inches

   Ⓘ   22 inches

Go On ▶

18 Gunter can run 3.2 miles in 30 minutes. How many feet would Gunter be able to run in 15 minutes? (1 mile = 5,280 feet)

19 Which number is a prime number?

    Ⓐ 9

    Ⓑ 12

    Ⓒ 19

    Ⓓ 49

20 Which measurements **best** describes the length of a car?

    Ⓕ 30 feet

    Ⓖ 300 inches

    Ⓗ 3 yards

    Ⓘ 3 feet

21 Which group of coordinates form a triangle with two congruent sides when plotted on a grid?

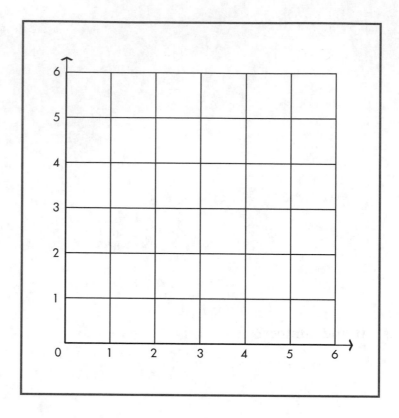

Ⓐ (2, 1); (4, 1); (2, 4)

Ⓑ (1, 1); (1, 3); (2, 3)

Ⓒ (2, 2); (4, 0); (4, 5)

Ⓓ (3, 4); (3, 2); (5, 2)

Go On ▶

22 The 4 fifth-grade classes at Nicholas Elementary School collected canned goods to donate to charity. Among the 4 classes, 540 cans were collected. Mr. Hale's class collected one third of the canned goods; Mrs. Filippetti's class collected 25% of the canned goods; Mrs. Beckett's class collected 20% of the canned goods; and Ms. Spears' class collected the remaining amount of canned goods.

Part A
Create a graph that displays each class's contribution to the canned-food drive. Be sure to label the graphs appropriately.

Part B
In the spaces provided, record the number of cans each class collected for the canned-food drive.

Number of cans collected by Mr. Hale's class: _____

Number of cans collected by Mrs. Filippetti's class: _____

Number of cans collected by Mrs. Beckett's class: _____

Number of cans collected by Ms. Spears' class: _____

23 The medal totals for the countries placing in the top 5 for the most medals at the 1996 Summer Olympics are listed in the table below.

1996 Summer Olympics Medal Counts			
Country	Gold	Silver	Bronze
U.S.A.	44	32	25
Germany	20	18	27
Russia	26	21	16
China	16	22	12
Australia	9	9	23

What was the **mean** number of gold medals received by these 5 countries?

Copying is Prohibited
© Englefield & Associates, Inc.

24 Several locations in Brokensword are mapped on the grid shown below.

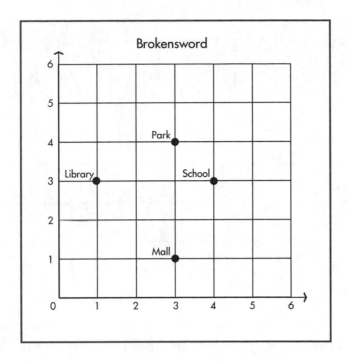

What is located at the coordinates (3, 4) on the map above?

- Ⓕ   the park
- Ⓖ   the mall
- Ⓗ   the school
- Ⓘ   the library

25 Give **three** names for the figure shown below.

THINK
SOLVE
EXPLAIN

_____

_____

_____

26 According to the graph below, what was the **median** temperature for May?

May Temperatures

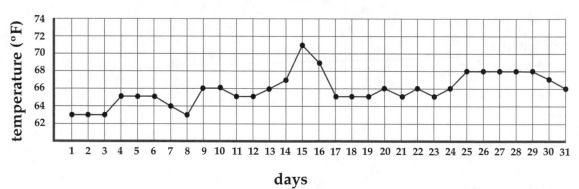

days

Ⓐ   65° F

Ⓑ   66° F

Ⓒ   67° F

Ⓓ   69° F

27 Hilda is sewing 8 new curtains for her bedroom windows. The length of each curtain is 4.75 feet.

THINK
SOLVE
EXPLAIN

On the lines below, ESTIMATE the length of fabric Hilda will need to complete her sewing project. Then, explain your estimate.

_____

_____

_____

_____

_____

_____

28 Sarah is 12 years old. She has a cousin, Kristin, who is 6 years older than half of Sarah's age. If Kristin's age is represented by n, which expression is correct?

F $n < 12$

G $n = 12$

H $n > 12$

I $n \geq 12$

29 Mr. Psamanthos is building his children a sandbox. He buys 24 feet of wood for the frame of the sandbox. If he builds a rectangular sandbox with one of the sides 8 feet in length, what will the area of the sandbox be in square feet? (Area = length x width)

```
┌──┬──┬──┬──┐
│  │  │  │  │
├──┼──┼──┼──┤
│0 │0 │0 │0 │
│1 │1 │1 │1 │
│2 │2 │2 │2 │
│3 │3 │3 │3 │
│4 │4 │4 │4 │
│5 │5 │5 │5 │
│6 │6 │6 │6 │
│7 │7 │7 │7 │
│8 │8 │8 │8 │
│9 │9 │9 │9 │
└──┴──┴──┴──┘
```

30 Jerome brought in 30 cupcakes to share with his class on his birthday. After he passed out 1 cupcake to each person in his class, he had 6 cupcakes remaining. What operation could Jerome use with this information to find out how many students are in his class?

ⓐ subtraction

ⓑ division

ⓒ addition

ⓓ multiplication

31 Sergei wants to find out what percent of people like to walk dogs. Which strategy should he use?

      Ⓕ   He should take a survey of people walking their dogs in the park.

      Ⓖ   He should take a survey of people at a pet store.

      Ⓗ   He should take a survey of people he chooses by looking in the phone book.

      Ⓘ   He should take a survey of people who don't own dogs to avoid bias.

32 Which instruments would you use to measure volume?

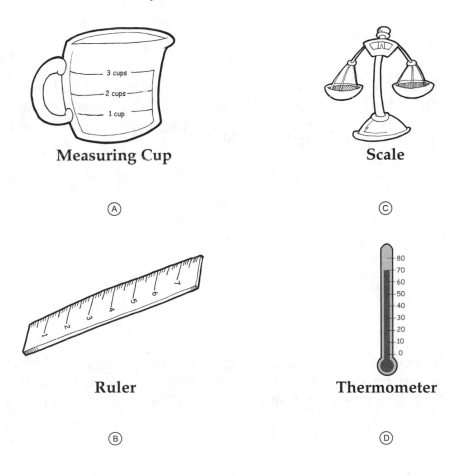

Measuring Cup

Ⓐ

Scale

Ⓒ

Ruler

Ⓑ

Thermometer

Ⓓ

33 What is the probability of rolling a number greater than 3 on a normal six-sided number cube?

F $\frac{1}{6}$

G $\frac{1}{3}$

H $\frac{1}{2}$

I $\frac{2}{3}$

34 At a skateboarding competition, each contestant was required to do 2 handplants during his or her half-pipe routine. If each of the 12 contestants did at least the required amount of handplants during his or her half-pipe routine, which expression represents the total number of handplants (n) done during the competition?

A $n = 24$

B $n > 24$

C $n \geq 24$

D $n < 24$

35 On every hour, the bells in the clock tower ring a number of times equal to the time. At 1:00 a.m., the bells ring once; at 2:00 a.m., the bells ring twice; at 3:00 a.m. the bells ring three times, etc. How many bells will ring between 5:45 a.m. and 8:50 a.m.?

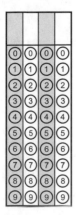

36 The table below shows the number of students in each grade at Perry Elementary School.

Grade	Students
Kindergarten	82
1st	119
2nd	100
3rd	96
4th	94
5th	119
6th	97

What is the **mean** number of students per grade at Perry Elementary School?

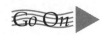

37 Stephanie will be 12 years old on her next birthday. Her sister Christy is 3 years older than she is. Oliver, Stephanie's brother, is 7 years younger than Christy. What is the current total age of Stephanie, Christy, and Oliver?

     Ⓕ 33 years

     Ⓖ 32 years

     Ⓗ 31 years

     Ⓘ 30 years

38 Which measurements **best** describes the height of a fire hydrant?

     Ⓐ 2 yards

     Ⓑ 4 feet

     Ⓒ 6 inches

     Ⓓ 18 inches

39 Manolo's mother asks him to go to the store and buy some eggs for a cake she is baking. On the way to the store, Manolo needs to stop at the library to return his library books.

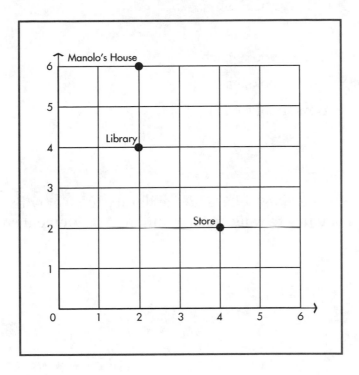

Which set of coordinates describes the trip to the store Manolo will take from point to point, beginning with his house?

Ⓕ (2, 6); (2, 4); (4, 2)

Ⓖ (6, 2); (4, 2); (2, 4)

Ⓗ (6, 2); (2, 4); (4, 2)

Ⓘ (2, 6); (4, 2); (2, 4)

40 Kelly has 24 comic books, which he wishes to put in folders. If he wants to put equal numbers of comic books in each folder, what is one way he could do so?

     Ⓐ   3 folders of 4 comic books each

     Ⓑ   2 folders of 12 comic books each

     Ⓒ   4 folders of 8 comic books each

     Ⓓ   6 folders of 5 comic books each

41 On Thursdays, Tina walks a few blocks to the library to meet with her tutor. Tina wants to measure how far she has to walk. Which unit of measurement should she use?

     Ⓕ   centimeters

     Ⓖ   inches

     Ⓗ   yards

     Ⓘ   miles

42 The school playground has a large square sandbox. One side of the sandbox measures 3 feet long. What is the **perimeter** of the sandbox in feet?

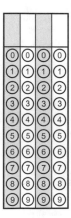

43 Which letter has only **one** line of symmetry?

     (A) H

     (B) Z

     (C) T

     (D) P

44 Which set of figures shows a **flip** or a **reflection**?

     (F)
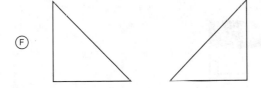

     (G)
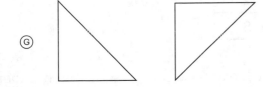

     (H)
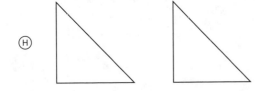

     (I)
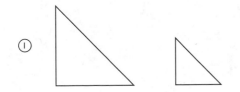

45 Carmen wants to trim the top of her supply box with stickers. If the top of her supply box measures 8 inches long by 4 inches wide, what is the **perimeter** of the box's top?

Ⓐ 4 inches

Ⓑ 8 inches

Ⓒ 12 inches

Ⓓ 24 inches

46 Study the "In" and "Out" table below.

IN	OUT
33	11
15	5
36	12
24	8

If *n* equals the number in the "In" column, which expression represents the number in the "Out" column?

Ⓕ $n > 6$

Ⓖ $n \times 3$

Ⓗ $n \div 3$

Ⓘ $n - 3$

Go On ▶

47 The Rosa family takes a vacation every summer. They use the chart below to figure out how much gasoline they need for their trip.

Miles Driven	Gallons of Gasoline used
20	.75
40	1.50
60	2.25
80	3.00
100	3.75
120	4.50
140	

Using the table above, determine the amount of gasoline the Rosas will need if they travel 140 miles. Then, explain your answer.

_____

_____

_____

_____

_____

_____

48 At the school festival, tickets are sold individually or at a discount in strips of 5. Micah bought 3 strips of tickets and her friend gave her 2 extra tickets. Now Micah has a total of 17 tickets.

If *t* equals the number of tickets in each strip, which of these equations describes Micah's tickets **best**?

Ⓐ $3t + 2 = 17$

Ⓑ $3t - 2 = 17$

Ⓒ $3t + 2t = 17$

Ⓓ $2t + 3 = 17$

49 Marco is using the stem-and-leaf plot below to keep track of the temperatures for June.

Stem	Leaf
5	0, 7, 9
6	1, 1, 2, 2, 4, 5, 5, 5, 7, 8, 9
7	0, 0, 1, 3, 6, 7, 9, 9
8	0, 0, 2, 2, 3, 7, 9

What is the **median** of the temperatures shown on the stem-and-leaf plot?

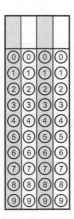

50 Richard is buying fish for his 50-gallon aquarium. The fish store tells him that he can have about 2 inches of fish per gallon of water. He knows that he would like 1 plecostomus, 8 neon tetras, 8 bloodfin tetras, and 2 blue gouramis.

Fish	Inches Per Fish
Plecostomus	5 inches
Neon Tetra	2 inches
Bloodfin Tetra	2 inches
Blue Gourami	4 inches

Using the chart above, how many inches of fish is Richard getting?

51 The table below shows the highest temperature in degrees Fahrenheit on 7 different days.

Sunday	83°
Monday	89°
Tuesday	94°
Wednesday	79°
Thursday	82°
Friday	85°
Saturday	77°

What is the **range** of these temperatures?

   Ⓕ 17°

   Ⓖ 18°

   Ⓗ 77°

   Ⓘ 89°

52 Which drawings show lines of symmetry?

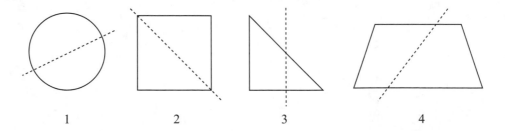

1   2   3   4

   Ⓐ 1 and 2

   Ⓑ 3 and 4

   Ⓒ 1 and 4

   Ⓓ 2 and 3

Go On ▶

53 Below is a map of Gerald's backyard. Each box on the grid measures 1 square yard. For his brother's pirate party, he has buried some things in the places shown on the map.

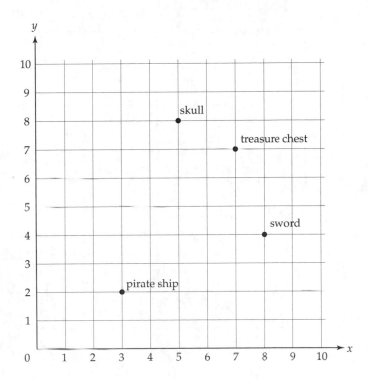

What are the coordinates for the pirate ship?

Ⓕ (2, 3)

Ⓖ (3, 2)

Ⓗ (7, 7)

Ⓘ (8, 4)

Go On ▶

54 What is located at $(\frac{7}{3}, 4)$ on the coordinate grid below?

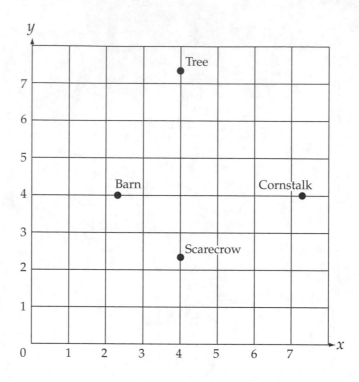

Ⓐ Tree

Ⓑ Barn

Ⓒ Scarecrow

Ⓓ Cornstalk

55 What is the **area** of the square below?

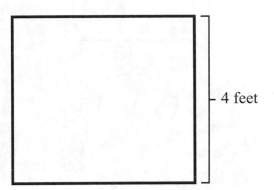

⌐ 4 feet

     Ⓕ   4 square feet

     Ⓖ   8 square feet

     Ⓗ 12 square feet

     Ⓘ 16 square feet

This is the end of the Mathematics Assessment.
Until time is called, go back and check your work or answer questions you did not complete. When you have finished, close your workbook.

Science

Introduction

This Assessment will ask you questions that test what you have learned so far in school. These questions are based on the science skills you have been taught in school through fifth grade. The questions you will answer are not meant to confuse or trick you but are written so you have the best chance to show what you know.

The *Show What You Know® on the 5th Grade FCAT, Student Workbook* includes a Science Practice Tutorial that will help you practice your test-taking skills. Following the Science Practice Tutorial is a full-length Science Assessment. Both the Science Practice Tutorial and the Science Assessment have been created to model the 5th Grade FCAT.

About the FCAT Science for Grade 5

The fifth-grade Science Assessment will test you on your understanding of eight science strands for fifth grade. This will include: the Nature of Matter, Energy, Force and Motion, Processes that Shape the Earth, Earth and Space, Processes of Life, How Living Things Interact with Their Environment, and the Nature of Science. The Science Assessment will have 55–60 multiple-choice, short-response, and extended-response questions.

Item Distribution and Scoring

The following chart shows the approximate percent of raw-score points taken from each Science Content Category.

Science Content Categories	Points
Physical and Chemical Sciences (Strands A, B, and C)	25%
Earth and Space Sciences (Strands D and E)	25%
Life and Environmental Sciences (Strands F and G)	25%
Scientific Thinking (Strand H)	25%

The FCAT Science will ask multiple-choice, short-response, and extended-response questions.

Science Item Type	Number of Items
Multiple Choice	45–55
Short and Extended Response	5–7
Total	50–55

Multiple-Choice Questions

On the fifth-grade FCAT, you will select from four possible answer choices and fill in a bubble. Although multiple-choice items sometimes ask for the recall of facts, most of the sample items demand a more complex thought process. Each multiple-choice item in the Assessment is scored 0 (incorrect) or 1 (correct). Each correct answer adds one point to the total Assessment score.

Short-Response Questions

Short-response items require you to generate your own answers—anything from a few words or numbers to several sentences. Many of these items ask you to explain your reasoning to support your answer. Short-response items are worth 2 points each and are scored according to the 2-point rubric below.

Two-Point Rubric for Short-Response Tasks

2 points	A score of two indicates that the student has demonstrated a thorough understanding of the scientific concepts and/or procedures embodied in the task. The student has completed the task correctly, in a scientifically sound manner. When required, student explanations and/or interpretations are clear and complete. The response may contain minor flaws that do not detract from the demonstration of a thorough understanding.
1 point	A score of one indicates that the student has provided a response that is only partially correct. For example, the student may arrive at an acceptable conclusion or provide an adequate interpretation, but may demonstrate some misunderstanding of the underlying scientific concepts and/or procedures. Conversely, a student may arrive at an unacceptable conclusion or provide a faulty interpretation, but could have applied appropriate and scientifically sound concepts and/or procedures.
0 points	A score of zero indicates that the student has not provided a response or has provided a response that does not demonstrate an understanding of the scientific concepts and/or procedures embodied in the task. The student's explanation may be uninterpretable, lack sufficient information to determine the student's understanding, contain clear misunderstandings of the underlying scientific concepts and/or procedures, or may be incorrect.

Extended-Response Questions

Extended-response items require a more developed response and may ask for an essay on a single topic or several short paragraphs in response to individual items. Virtually every extended-response item will demand higher-level thinking skills. Many students offer very minimal written responses (3 words instead of 3 paragraphs). Good performance requires practice in writing full, well-supported responses. Extended-response items are worth 4 points each and are scored according to the 4-point rubric below.

Four-Point Rubric for Extended-Response Tasks

4 points	A score of four indicates that the student has demonstrated a thorough understanding of the scientific concepts and/or procedures embodied in the task. The student has completed the task correctly, used scientifically sound procedures, and provided clear and complete explanations and interpretations. The response may contain minor flaws that do not detract from a demonstration of a thorough understanding.
3 points	A score of three indicates that the student has demonstrated an understanding of the scientific concepts and/or procedures embodied in the task. The student's response to the task is essentially correct, but the scientific procedures, explanations, and/or interpretations provided are not thorough. The response may contain minor flaws that reflect inattentiveness or indicate some misunderstanding of the underlying scientific concepts and/or procedures.
2 points	A score of two indicates that the student has demonstrated only a partial understanding of the scientific concepts and/or procedures embodied in the task. Although the student may have arrived at an acceptable conclusion or provided an adequate interpretation of the task, the student's work lacks an essential understanding of the underlying scientific concepts and/or procedures. The response may contain errors related to misunderstanding important aspects of the task, misuse of scientific procedures/processes, or faulty interpretations of results.
1 points	A score of one indicates that the student has demonstrated a very limited understanding of the scientific concepts and/or procedures embodied in the task. The student's response is incomplete and exhibits many flaws. Although the student's response has addressed some of the conditions of the task, the student has reached an inadequate conclusion and/or provided reasoning that is faulty or incomplete. The response exhibits many flaws or may be incomplete.
0 points	A score of zero indicates that the student has not provided a response or has provided a response that does not demonstrate an understanding of the scientific concepts and/or procedures embodied in the task. The student's explanation may be uninterpretable, lack sufficient information to determine the student's understanding, contain clear misunderstandings of the underlying scientific concepts and/or procedures, or may be incorrect.

"Read, Inquire, Explain" Questions

 This symbol appears next to questions that require short written answers. Use about 5 minutes to answer these questions. A complete and correct answer to each of these questions is worth 2 points. A partially correct answer is worth 1 point.

 This symbol appears next to questions that require longer written answers. Use about 10 to 15 minutes to answer these questions. A complete and correct answer to each of these questions is worth 4 points. A partially correct answer is worth 1, 2, or 3 points.

How to Answer the "Read, Inquire, Explain" Questions

Answers to the short- and extended-response problems can receive full or partial credit. You should try to answer these questions even if you are not sure of the correct answer. If a portion of the answer is correct, you will get a portion of the points.

- Allow about 5 minutes to answer the short "Read, Inquire, Explain" questions and about 10 to 15 minutes to answer the long ones.

- Read the question carefully.

- If you do not understand the question, read it again and try to answer one part at a time.

- Be sure to answer every part of the question.

- Show your work. This shows that you understand how to solve the problem.

- Reread your explanation to make sure it says what you want it to say.

Hints to Remember for Taking the FCAT Science Test

Here are some hints to help you do your best when you take the FCAT Science test. Keep these hints in mind when you answer the sample questions.

- Learn how to answer each kind of question. The FCAT Science test for Grade 5 has three types of questions: multiple-choice, short-response, and extended-response.

- Read each question carefully.

- Check each answer to make sure it is the best answer for the question.

- Answer the questions you are sure about first. If a question seems too difficult, skip it and go back to it later.

- Be sure to fill in the answer bubbles correctly. Do not make any stray marks around answer spaces.

- Think positively. Some questions may seem hard to you, but you may be able to figure out what to do if you reread the question carefully.

- When you have finished each question, reread it to make sure your answer is reasonable.

- Relax. Some people get nervous about tests. It's natural. Just do your best.

Periodic Table of Elements

Key:
Atomic Number — 1
Symbol — H
Atomic Mass — 1.008
Name — Hydrogen

Group 1 / 1A	2 / 2A	3 / 3B	4 / 4B	5 / 5B	6 / 6B	7 / 7B	8 / 8B	9 / 8B	10 / 8B	11 / 1B	12 / 2B	13 / 3A	14 / 4A	15 / 5A	16 / 6A	17 / 7A	18 / 8A
1 **H** 1.008 Hydrogen																	2 **He** 4.0026 Helium
3 **Li** 6.941 Lithium	4 **Be** 9.012 Beryllium											5 **B** 10.81 Boron	6 **C** 12.011 Carbon	7 **N** 14.007 Nitrogen	8 **O** 15.999 Oxygen	9 **F** 18.998 Fluorine	10 **Ne** 20.179 Neon
11 **Na** 22.990 Sodium	12 **Mg** 24.305 Magnesium											13 **Al** 26.982 Aluminum	14 **Si** 28.086 Silicon	15 **P** 30.974 Phosphorus	16 **S** 32.066 Sulfur	17 **Cl** 35.453 Chlorine	18 **Ar** 39.948 Argon
19 **K** 39.098 Potassium	20 **Ca** 40.08 Calcium	21 **Sc** 44.956 Scandium	22 **Ti** 47.88 Titanium	23 **V** 50.942 Vanadium	24 **Cr** 51.996 Chromium	25 **Mn** 54.938 Manganese	26 **Fe** 55.847 Iron	27 **Co** 58.933 Cobalt	28 **Ni** 58.69 Nickel	29 **Cu** 63.546 Copper	30 **Zn** 65.39 Zinc	31 **Ga** 69.72 Gallium	32 **Ge** 72.61 Germanium	33 **As** 74.922 Arsenic	34 **Se** 78.96 Selenium	35 **Br** 79.904 Bromine	36 **Kr** 83.80 Krypton
37 **Rb** 85.468 Rubidium	38 **Sr** 87.62 Strontium	39 **Y** 88.906 Yttrium	40 **Zr** 91.224 Zirconium	41 **Nb** 92.906 Niobium	42 **Mo** 95.94 Molybdenum	43 **Tc** (98) Technetium	44 **Ru** 101.07 Ruthenium	45 **Rh** 102.906 Rhodium	46 **Pd** 106.42 Palladium	47 **Ag** 107.868 Silver	48 **Cd** 112.41 Cadmium	49 **In** 114.82 Indium	50 **Sn** 118.71 Tin	51 **Sb** 121.763 Antimony	52 **Te** 127.60 Tellurium	53 **I** 126.904 Iodine	54 **Xe** 131.29 Xenon
55 **Cs** 132.905 Cesium	56 **Ba** 137.33 Barium	57 **La** 138.906 Lanthanum	72 **Hf** 178.49 Hafnium	73 **Ta** 180.948 Tantalum	74 **W** 183.84 Tungsten	75 **Re** 186.207 Rhenium	76 **Os** 190.23 Osmium	77 **Ir** 192.22 Iridium	78 **Pt** 195.08 Platinum	79 **Au** 196.967 Gold	80 **Hg** 200.59 Mercury	81 **Tl** 204.383 Thallium	82 **Pb** 207.2 Lead	83 **Bi** 208.980 Bismuth	84 **Po** (209) Polonium	85 **At** (210) Astatine	86 **Rn** (222) Radon
87 **Fr** (223) Francium	88 **Ra** 226.025 Radium	89 **Ac** 227.028 Actinium	104 **Rf** (261) Rutherfordium	105 **Db** (262) Dubnium	106 **Sg** (263) Seaborgium	107 **Bh** (262) Bohrium	108 **Hs** (265) Hassium	109 **Mt** (266) Meitnerium									

Transition Metals · Inner Transition Metals

Lanthanide series

58 **Ce** 140.12 Cerium	59 **Pr** 140.908 Praseodymium	60 **Nd** 144.24 Neodymium	61 **Pm** (145) Promethium	62 **Sm** 150.36 Samarium	63 **Eu** 151.97 Europium	64 **Gd** 157.25 Gadolinium	65 **Tb** 158.925 Terbium	66 **Dy** 162.50 Dysprosium	67 **Ho** 164.930 Holmium	68 **Er** 167.26 Erbium	69 **Tm** 168.934 Thulium	70 **Yb** 173.04 Ytterbium	71 **Lu** 174.967 Lutetium

Actinide series

90 **Th** 232.038 Thorium	91 **Pa** 231.036 Protactinium	92 **U** 238.029 Uranium	93 **Np** 237.048 Neptunium	94 **Pu** (244) Plutonium	95 **Am** (243) Americium	96 **Cm** (247) Curium	97 **Bk** (247) Berkelium	98 **Cf** (251) Californium	99 **Es** (252) Einsteinium	100 **Fm** (257) Fermium	101 **Md** (258) Mendelevium	102 **No** (259) Nobelium	103 **Lr** (262) Lawrencium

Nonmetals · Metals

Glossary

absorb: To suck up or drink in (a liquid); soak up; to take up or receive by chemical or molecular action.

adaptation: A change that allows an organism to become better suited for survival in its environment.

affect: To act on; produce an effect or change in.

air: The mixture of gases, mainly nitrogen and oxygen, that forms Earth's atmosphere.

amount: A quantity or degree of something, considered as a unit or total.

amount of time: The measurement of how long it takes to do something.

apply: The skill of selecting and using information in other situations or problems.

atmosphere: The gaseous layers that encircle the Earth and other planets.

atom: The smallest particle of an element that can exist either alone or in combination.

axis: An imaginary straight line around which an object, such as Earth, rotates.

balance scale: An accurate device used to measure the weight of chemicals and other substances.

bone: Hard tissue that forms the skeleton of the body in vertebrate animals.

brain: The controlling center of the nervous system in vertebrates, connected to the spinal cord and enclosed in the cranium; a nervous-system center in some invertebrates that is functionally similar to the brain in vertebrates.

carnivore: A flesh-eating animal.

cause: (v) To make something happen or exist or be the reason that somebody does something or something happens; (n) something that, or somebody who, makes something happen or exist, or is responsible for a certain result.

cell: The smallest unit of living matter capable of functioning independently.

centimeter (cm): A metric unit of length equal to one hundredth of a meter.

characteristic: A feature or quality that makes somebody or something recognizable.

chart: A diagram or table displaying detailed information.

chemical change: A change in a substance resulting in an entirely different substance with different properties from the first.

classify: To assign things or people to classes or groups.

climate: The average weather or the regular variations in weather in a region over a period of years.

color: The property of objects that depends on the light that they reflect and that is perceived as red, blue, green, or other shades.

community: Interacting populations that live in a defined habitat.

compost: A mixture of decayed plants and other organic matter used by gardeners for enriching soil.

Glossary

compound: A substance formed from two or more elements chemically united in fixed proportions.

conclude: (v) To form an opinion or make a logical judgment about something after considering everything known about it.

conclusion: A decision made or an opinion formed after considering the relevant facts or evidence.

condensation: The process by which atmospheric water vapor liquifies to form fog, clouds, or the like, or solidifies to form snow or hail.

condense: (v) To lose heat and change from a vapor into a liquid, or to make a vapor change to a liquid.

conserve: To use something sparingly so as not to exhaust supplies.

conservation: A law that states that matter and/or energy in a closed system are constant.

constellation: A group of stars that form a recognizable pattern and are often named after their shape or mythological figure.

consumer: In an ecological community or food chain, an organism that feeds on other organisms, or on material derived from them.

conversion: A change in the nature, form, or function of something.

continent: Any one of the seven large continuous land masses that constitute most of the dry land on the surface of Earth.

cycle: A sequence of events that is repeated again and again.

data: Information, often in the form of facts or figures obtained from experiments or surveys, used as a basis for making calculations or drawing conclusions.

decomposer: An organism, especially a bacterium or fungus, that causes organic matter to rot or decay.

demonstrate: To show or prove something clearly and convincingly.

density: The degree of compactness of a substance.

depend: To be affected or decided by other factors.

deposition: The natural process of laying down matter, such as sediments in a river.

describe: The skill of developing a detailed picture, image, or characterization using diagrams and/or words, written, or oral.

design: The application of scientific concepts and principles and the inquiry process to the solution of human problems that regularly provide tools to further investigate the natural world.

diagram: A simple drawing showing the basic shape, layout, or workings of something.

diameter: A straight line running from one side of a circle or other rounded geometric figure through the center to the other side, or the length of this line; the width or thickness of something, especially something circular or cylindrical.

direction: The management or control of somebody or something by providing instructions.

Glossary

Earth: The third planet in order from the sun with an orbital period of 365.26 days, a diameter of 12,756 km/7,926 mi, and an average distance from the sun of 149,600,000 km/ 93,000,000 mi.

earthquake: A violent shaking of Earth's crust that may cause destruction to buildings and installations and results from the sudden release of tectonic stress along a fault line or volcanic activity.

echo: The repetition of a sound caused by the reflection of sound waves from a surface.

ecosystem: A localized group of interdependent organisms together with the environment that they inhabit and depend on.

effect: The result or consequence of an action, influence, or causal agent.

egg: A large sex cell produced by birds, fish, insects, reptiles, or amphibians, enclosed in a protective covering that allows the fertilized embryo to continue developing outside the mother's body until it hatches; a female reproductive cell.

electrical: Caused by electricity or something that uses or conveys electricity.

electricity: A fundamental form of kinetic or potential energy created by the free or controlled movement of charged particles such as electrons, positrons, and ions.

element: Any of more than 100 fundamental substances that consist of atoms of only one kind and that singly or in combination constitute all matter.

energy: The ability or power to work or make an effort.

energy of motion (kinetic): The energy that a body or system has because of its motion.

energy pyramid: A diagram to help visualize how and where energy moves through living organisms in the food chain.

energy transfer: A change from one form of energy to another form of energy.

environment: The complex of physical, chemical, and biotic factors that act upon an organism or an ecological community and ultimately determine its form and survival.

equator: An imaginary line around the Earth's surface that is equal distances between the poles and divides the Earth into two hemispheres.

erode: To wear away outer layers of rock or soil, or to be gradually worn away by the action of wind or water.

erosion: The gradual wearing away of rock or soil by physical breakdown, chemical solution, and transportation of material, as caused, for example, by water, wind, or ice.

eruption: The violent ejection of material, such as gas, steam, ash, or lava from a volcano.

evaporate: To change a liquid into a vapor, usually by heating to below its boiling point, or to change from a liquid to vapor in this way.

evaporation: A process in which something is changed from a liquid to a vapor without its temperature reaching the boiling point.

event: A happening or occurrence.

evidence: Observations, measurements, or data collected through established and recognized scientific processes.

Glossary

experiment: A test or trial carried out under controlled conditions, in order to prove a theory or hypothesis.

explain: The skill of making a theory, hypothesis, inference, or conclusion plain and comprehensible—includes supporting details with an example.

explanation: The giving of details about something or reasons for something.

feet: Plural for foot; one foot is a unit of length in the U.S. Customary and British Imperial systems equal to .3048 m (12 inches). There are three feet in a yard.

flower: A colored, sometimes scented, part of a plant that contains the plant's reproductive organ.

food: Material that provides living things with the nutrients they need for energy and growth.

food chain: A hierarchy of different living things, each of which feeds on the one below.

food web (food cycle): The totality of interacting food chains in an ecological community; interacting food chains in an ecological community.

force: The power, strength, or energy that somebody or something possesses; a physical influence that tends to change the position of an object with mass, equal to the rate of change in momentum of the object: symbol *F*.

forest: A large area of land covered in trees and other plants growing close together, or the trees growing on it.

fossil: The remains of an animal or plant preserved from an earlier era inside a rock or other geological deposit, often as an impression or in a petrified state.

freeze: To be changed, or cause liquid to change, into a solid by the loss of heat, especially to change water into ice; to harden, or cause something to harden, through the effects of cold or frost.

friction: The rubbing of two objects against each other when one or both are moving.

fulcrum: The point of support on which a lever turns or pivots.

function: An action or use for which something is suited or designed.

galaxy: Any of the very large groups of stars and associated matter that are found throughout the universe.

gas: A substance, such as air, that is neither a solid nor a liquid at ordinary temperatures and that has the ability to expand indefinitely.

germinate: To start to grow from a seed or spore into a new individual; to be created and start to develop.

glacier: A large body of continuously accumulating ice and compacted snow, formed in mountain valleys or at the poles, that deforms under its own weight and slowly moves.

gram (g): A metric unit of mass, equal to 0.001 kg or equivalent to approximately 0.035 oz.

Glossary

graph: A diagram used to indicate relationships between two or more variable quantities. The quantities are measured along two axes, usually at right angles.

grassland: Land on which grass or low green plants are the main vegetation.

gravitation: A gradual and steady movement to or toward somebody or something as if drawn by some force or attraction; the mutual force of attraction between all particles or bodies that have mass.

gravity: The attraction due to gravitation that the Earth or another celestial body exerts on an object on or near its surface.

habitat: The place or environment where a plant or animal naturally or normally lives and grows.

hand lens: A magnifying glass with a handle for holding in the hand.

hardness: The state or quality of being firm, solid, and compact; the degree to which a metal may be scratched, abraded, indented, or machined, measured according to any of several scales.

heart: A hollow muscular organ that pumps blood around the body, in humans situated in the center of the chest with its apex directed to the left.

heat: Energy transfer that results from a difference in temperature between a system and its surroundings or between two parts of the same system.

heat energy: A form of transferred energy that arises from the random motion of molecules and is felt as temperature, especially as warmth or hotness.

herbivore: A plant-eating animal.

identify: To recognize somebody or something and to be able to say who or what he, she, or it is.

igneous rock: The cooled and hardened form of molten magma that generally reaches the Earth's surface as a result of volcanic activity.

inch (in.): A unit of length equal to 2.54 cm or 1/12th of a foot.

inclined plane: A surface set at an angle to the horizontal; a simple machine to raise or lower objects.

inertia: The tendency of a body at rest to remain at rest, or a body in motion in a straight line to remain in motion in a straight line, unless acted on by an outside force.

inherited: To receive a characteristic or quality as a result of its being passed on genetically.

input: The addition of matter, energy, or information to a system; a change of matter or energy in the system; a living organism learning something new.

inquiry: The skill of the investigative process characterized by asking questions of the natural world, developing hypotheses, testing hypotheses by manipulating variables and measuring responding variables, and drawing inferences from data to develop correlations between variables or cause-effect relationships between variables.

invent: To create something.

invention: Something that someone has created, especially a device or process.

Glossary

investigate: To carry out a detailed examination or inquiry in order to find out about something.

investigation: A multifaceted and organized scientific study of the natural world that involves making observations; asking questions; gathering information through planned study in the field, laboratory, or research setting; and using tools to gather data that is analyzed to find patterns and is subsequently communicated.

kilogram (kg): The basic unit of mass in the SI system, equal to 1,000 grams or 2.2046 lbs.

kilometer (km): The basic unit of measurement in the SI system, equal to 1,000 meters or 0.621 miles.

kinetic energy: Energy associated with motion.

lake: A large body of water surrounded by land.

leaf: Any of the flat green parts that grow in various shapes from the stems or branches of plants and trees; its main function is photosynthesis.

learned (acquired) characteristic: A characteristic that an organism develops in response to its environment and that cannot be passed on to the next generation.

lever: A rigid bar that pivots about a point (fulcrum) and is used to move or lift a load at one end by applying force to the other end.

life cycle: The series of stages in form and functional activity through which an organism grows and develops.

light: Electromagnetic radiation that can be seen by the human eye.

liquid: A substance in a condition in which it flows, that is a fluid at room temperature and atmospheric pressure, and in which shape, but not volume, can be changed.

liter (L): A unit of volume equal to 1 cubic decimeter or 1.056 liquid quarts.

living: Alive, not dead.

logical plan: An investigative plan that has coherence among all its attributes, including hypotheses, observations and data to support the hypotheses, and logical inference to support conclusions.

lung: In air-breathing vertebrate animals, either of the paired spongy respiratory organs, situated inside the rib cage, that transfer oxygen into the blood and remove carbon dioxide from it.

machine: A device with moving parts, often powered by electricity, used to perform a task, especially one that would otherwise be done by hand.

magnetic: Able to attract iron or steel objects.

magnifying glass: A convex lens in a frame with a handle, used to make objects viewed through it appear larger.

mass: The property of an object that is a measure of its inertia, the amount of matter it contains, and its influence in a gravitational field: symbol m.

material: Relating to or consisting of solid physical matter.

matter: The material substance of the universe that has mass, occupies space, and is convertible to energy.

Glossary

melt: To change a substance from a solid to a liquid state by heating it, or be changed in this way.

metamorphic rock: A rock that has changed in constitution, because of pressure, heat, or water, resulting in a more compact and more highly crystalline condition.

meter (m): The basic SI unit of length, equivalent to approximately 1.094 yd or 39.37 in.

microscopic: A condition in which an object cannot be seen without the use of a microscope.

mile (mi): A unit of linear measurement on land equivalent to 5,280 ft or 1,760 yd or 1.6 km.

milliliter (mL): A unit of volume equal to one thousandth of a liter.

mineral: An inorganic substance that must be ingested by animals or plants in order to remain healthy. For example, the minerals that a plant takes from the soil or the constituents in food that keep a human body healthy and help it grow.

mixture: A portion of matter consisting of two or more components in varying proportions that retain their own properties.

model: A representation of a system, subsystem, or parts of a system that can be used to predict or demonstrate the operation or qualities of the system.

molecule: The smallest physical unit of a substance that can exist independently, consisting of one or more atoms held together by chemical forces.

moon: Earth's only natural satellite; the astronomical body nearest to Earth, except for some artificial satellites and occasional meteors.

moon phase: Referring to the portion of the Moon that is illuminated, as seen from Earth; the phases: new moon, waxing crescent, first quarter, waxing gibbous, full moon, waning gibbous, last quarter, and waning crescent.

mountain: A high and often rocky area of a land mass with steep or sloping sides.

muscle: A tissue that is specialized to undergo repeated contraction and relaxation, thereby producing movement of body parts, maintaining tension, or pumping fluids within the body.

newton (N): An SI unit of force equivalent to the force that produces an acceleration of one meter per second on a mass of one kilogram.

nonliving: Not containing or supporting life.

nonrenewable resource: A natural resource that cannot be re-grown or regenerated, and exists in a fixed amount.

nutrient (mineral): Any substance that provides nourishment; for example, the minerals that a plant takes from the soil or the constituents in food that keep a human body healthy and help it grow.

object: Something that can be seen or touched.

observe: To watch someone or something attentively, especially for scientific purposes.

observation: The skill of recognizing and noting some fact or occurrence in the natural world, including the act of measuring.

Glossary

ocean: A large expanse of salt water, especially any of Earth's five largest such areas: the Atlantic, Pacific, Indian, Arctic, and Antarctic oceans.

orbit: (n) The path that a celestial body, such as a planet, moon, or satellite follows around a larger celestial body, such as the sun; (v) To move around a celestial body in a path dictated by the force of gravity exerted by that body.

organ: A structure (such as a heart, kidney, leaf, or stem) consisting of cells and tissues, and performing some specific function in an organism.

organism: A living thing, such as a plant, animal, or bacterium.

organize: To arrange the elements of something in a way that creates a particular structure.

ounce: A unit of weight equal to one-sixteenth of a pound; a unit for measuring liquid, equal to 0.0284 of a liter.

output: The removal of matter, energy, or information from a system; a change of matter or energy in the system; a living organism produces and excretes a substance.

oxygen: A colorless, odorless gas that is the most abundant chemical element and forms compounds with most others: symbol O.

part: Any of several equal portions that make up something, such as a mixture.

pattern: A regular or repetitive form, order, or arrangement.

photosynthesis: The chemical process by which chlorophyll-containing plants use light to convert carbon dioxide and water into carbohydrates, releasing oxygen as a by-product.

physical change: A change in a substance that does not alter its chemical makeup.

pitch: The level of a sound in the scale, defined by its frequency.

plan: A method of doing something that is worked out usually in some detail before it is begun and that may be written down in some form or simply retained in memory.

planet: An astronomical body that orbits a star and does not shine with its own light, especially one of the nine such bodies orbiting the sun in the solar system.

pollute: To cause harm to an area of the natural environment, for example, the air, soil, or water, usually by introducing damaging substances, such as chemicals or waste products.

population: All the plants or animals of the same kind found in a given area.

potential energy: The energy that matter has because of its position or because of the arrangement of atoms or parts.

pound (lb): A unit of weight divided into 16 ounces and equivalent to 0.45 kg.

precipitation: Rain, snow, or hail, all of which are formed by condensation of moisture in the atmosphere and fall to the ground.

predator: An animal that lives by capturing prey as a means of maintaining life.

Glossary

predict: To say what is going to happen in the future, often on the basis of present indications or past experience.

prediction: The skill of predicting a future event or process based on theory, investigation, or experience.

prey: An animal taken by a predator as food.

problem: A question or puzzle that needs to be solved.

procedure: An established or correct method of doing something.

process: A series of actions directed toward a particular aim; a series of natural occurrences that produce change or development.

producer: An organism, such as a green plant, that manufactures its own food from simple inorganic substances.

property: A characteristic quality or distinctive feature of something (often used in the plural form: properties).

properties: The basic or essential attributes shared by all members of a group.

protist: Organisms that are unicellular, or multicellular without specialized tissues, that belong to the kingdom Protista.

pull: To apply force to a physical object so as to draw or tend to draw it toward the force's origin.

pulley: A mounted rotating wheel with a grooved rim over which a belt or chain can move to change the direction of a pulling force.

push: The act of applying pressure or force to somebody or something in order to move that person or object.

question: A problem to be discussed or solved in an examination or experiment.

radius: A straight line extending from the center of a circle to its edge or from the center of a sphere to its surface: symbol *r*.

rate: The speed at which one measured quantity happens, runs, moves, or changes compared to another measured amount, such as time.

recycle: To process used or waste material so that it can be used again.

reduce: To become or make something smaller in size, number, extent, degree, or intensity.

reflection: The throwing back by a body or surface of light, heat, or sound without absorbing it.

refraction: Deflection from a straight path by a light ray or energy wave in passing from one medium (such as air) to another (such as glass) in which its velocity is different.

renewable resource: A natural resource that does not decrease in supply; it is replenished by natural processes over time.

report: To give detailed information about research or an investigation.

reproduce: To produce offspring or new individuals through a sexual or asexual process.

Glossary

reproduction: The production of young plants and animals of the same kind through a sexual or asexual process.

resource: Industrial materials and capabilities supplied by nature; substances used by an organism for survival.

result: To produce a particular outcome.

river: A natural formation in which fresh water forms a wide stream that runs across the land until it reaches the sea or another body of water.

root: The part of a plant that has no leaves or buds and usually spreads underground, anchoring the plant and absorbing water and nutrients from the soil.

scavenger: An animal, bird, or other organism that feeds on dead and rotting flesh or discarded food scraps.

science: The systematized knowledge of the natural world derived from observation, study, and investigation; also the activity of specialists to add to the body of this knowledge.

scientific: Relating to, using, or conforming to science or its principles; proceeding in a systematic and methodical way.

scientific method: Principles and procedures for the systemic pursuit of knowledge involving the recognition and formulation of a problem, the collection of data through observation and experiment, and the formulation and testing of hypotheses.

scientist: Somebody who has had scientific training or who works in one of the sciences.

sea: The great body of salt water that covers a large portion of Earth.

sediment: Material eroded from pre-existing rocks that is transported by water, wind, or ice and deposited elsewhere.

sedimentary rock: A rock formed by the deposition of sediment, affected by water, wind, or ice patterns, or by chemical combinations.

seed: The body, produced by reproduction in most plants, that contains the embryo and gives rise to a new individual. In flowering plants, it is enclosed within the fruit.

shadow: Relative darkness in a place that is being screened or blocked off from direct sunlight.

shape: The outline of something's form.

size: The amount, scope, or degree of something, in terms of how large or small it is.

skeleton: The rigid framework of interconnected bones and cartilage that protects and supports the internal organs and provides attachment for muscles in humans and other vertebrate animals.

skepticism: The attitude in scientific thinking that emphasizes that no fact or principle can be known with complete certainty; the theory that all knowledge is uncertain.

soil: The top layer of most of Earth's land surface, consisting of the unconsolidated products of rock erosion and organic decay, along with bacteria and fungi.

solar: Relating to or originating from the sun.

Glossary

solar system: A region in space where celestial bodies (planets and moons) orbit a star.

solid: Consisting of compact unyielding material having no open interior spaces; not hollow.

solve: To find a way of dealing successfully with a problem or difficulty.

sort: To arrange data in a set order.

sound: Vibrations traveling through air, water, or some other medium, especially those within the range of frequencies that can be perceived by the human ear.

special: Designed or reserved for a particular purpose.

speed: The rate at which something moves, happens, or functions.

spin (rotate): To turn or make something turn round and round rapidly, as if on an axis.

spring scale: A balance that measures weight by the tension on a spiral spring.

sprout: To begin to grow from a seed; a new growth on a plant; for example, a bud or shoot.

star: A natural luminous body visible in the sky, especially at night.

states of matter: The three traditional states of matter are solids, liquids, and gases.

stem: The main axis of a plant that bears buds and shoots.

stream: A narrow and shallow river; a current of air or water.

strength: The ability to withstand force, pressure, or stress.

structure: A part of a body or organism; for example, an organ or tissue, identifiable by its shape and other properties.

substance: A particular kind of matter or material.

summary: A shortened version of something that has been said or written, containing only the main points.

sun: The star at the center of our solar system around which Earth and the seven other planets orbit. It provides us with heat and light.

system: An assemblage of inter-related parts or conditions through which matter, energy, and information flow.

table: An arrangement of information or data into columns and rows or a condensed list.

temperature: The heat of something measured on a particular scale, such as the Fahrenheit or Celsius scale: symbol T.

texture: The feel and appearance of a surface, especially how rough or smooth it is.

thaw: To melt or make something melt.

thermometer: An instrument for measuring temperature; for example, an instrument with a graduated glass tube and a bulb containing mercury or alcohol that rises in the tube when the temperature increases.

Glossary

tissue: A mass of cells usually of a particular kind together with their intercellular substance that form one of the structural materials of organisms.

tool: Instruments or utensils that are used to do a particular job.

topography: The surface features of a given land area, with relative positions and elevations indicated.

transfer: The movement of energy from one location in a system to another system or subsystem.

universe: All matter and energy, as a whole.

vapor: Moisture or some other matter visible in the air as mist, clouds, fumes, or smoke.

variable: Something capable of changing or varying.

versus (v): As opposed to or contrasted with.

vibration: An instance of shaking or moving back and forth very rapidly.

volcano: A naturally occurring opening in the surface of Earth through which molten, gaseous, and solid material is ejected.

volume: The loudness of a sound; the size of a three-dimensional space enclosed within or occupied by an object: symbol V.

waste: The undigested remainder of food expelled from the body.

water: The clear liquid, essential for all plant and animal life, that occurs as rain, snow, and ice, and forms rivers, lakes, and seas.

water cycle: The sequence of conditions through which water passes from vapor in the atmosphere to precipitation upon land or water surfaces and ultimately back into the atmosphere as a result of evaporation and transpiration.

weather: The state of the atmosphere with regard to temperature, cloudiness, rainfall, wind, and other meteorological conditions.

weathering: To be worn, damaged, or seasoned by exposure to the weather; used to describe the process by which rocks are eroded or changed by the action of the weather.

weight: The heaviness of somebody or something.

wheel and axle: A simple machine where a circular disk turns a central axis, or vice versa.

wind: Air in motion.

BLANK PAGE

Science
Practice Tutorial

Directions for Taking the Science Practice Tutorial

The Science Practice Tutorial contains 43 practice questions. You will mark your answers in this book. If you don't understand a question, just ask your teacher to explain it to you.

This section will review the Strands, Standards, and Benchmarks used to assess student achievement in the state of Florida. Following the description of each Benchmark, a sample Science practice item is given. Each item gives you an idea of how the Benchmark may be assessed. Review these items to increase your familiarity with FCAT-style multiple-choice, short-response, and extended-response items. Once you have read through this Practice Tutorial section, you will be ready to complete the full-length Science Assessment.

Sample Multiple-Choice Item

To help you understand how to answer the test questions, look at the sample test question below. It is included to show you what a multiple-choice item in the test is like and how to mark your answer.

1 The prickly pear cactus is easy to recognize because of its large, long sharp spines. Another characteristic of this species is its large, bright yellow flowers. What is an additional characteristic that is **true** of the prickly pear cactus?

Ⓐ The cactus can only grow to be three centimeters tall.

Ⓑ The cactus needs large amounts of water to survive.

● The cactus can survive with limited water.

Ⓓ The cactus does not rely on sunlight for photosynthesis.

For this sample question, the correct choice is Answer C "The cactus can survive with limited water." Therefore, the circle next to Answer C is filled in.

Copying is Prohibited   © Englefield & Associates, Inc.

Sample Short-Response Item

To help you understand how to answer the test questions, look at the sample test question below. It is included to show you what a short-response item in the test is like and how to write your answer.

---

2 A student uses a plant, a piece of paper, and paper clips to perform an experiment. She uses paper clips to secure the sheet of paper around one leaf of the plant. The piece of paper is left there for two weeks.

What **most likely** happened to the leaf after two weeks? Explain your answer.

Most likely the leaf turned yellow and dropped off of the plant.
Plants need water, sunlight, and air to grow and live. If denied
sunlight, that part of the plant will die.

What **most likely** happened to the other leaves on the plant? Explain your answer.

Most likely the other leaves on the plant were still green and
thriving because they received water, sunlight, and air.

Sample Extended-Response Item

To help you understand how to answer the test questions, look at the sample test question below. It is included to show you what an extended-response item in the test is like and how to write your answer.

3 Matthew collected eight frog tadpoles from a pond near his house. He wants to find out how long it takes for the tadpoles to go through each of the stages below.

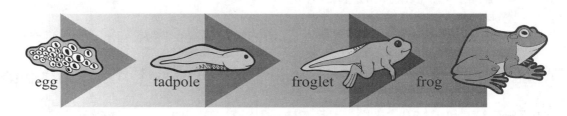

egg   tadpole   froglet   frog

Design a procedure Matthew could follow to find out how long each stage will last.

1) Create an environment that will allow the tadpoles to get the nutrients needed to survive and grow (a small aquarium, pond water from where the tadpoles were found, and plantlife or algae).

2) Keep a journal. Note changes that you see every day.

3) Take photographs. If you have a camera and are able to take pictures, place the pictures in the journal when you are finished. These photos could be very helpful with the final results of the inv·stigation.

4) Repeat the investigation several times.

5) Compare the data.

Science Practice Tutorial

1 The thermometer below shows the temperature in the school cafeteria in degrees Fahrenheit.

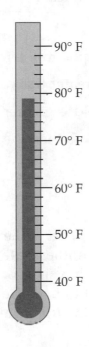

What is the temperature?

Ⓐ 79° C

Ⓑ 78° C

Ⓒ 78° F

Ⓓ 79° F

2 Ariana's grandfather makes candies. Using his special recipe, he mixes several ingredients in a pan and places the pan over a burner that is set to medium heat. He carefully stirs the liquid. Then he pours the liquid into candy molds. As the candies cool, they become solid. Ariana's grandfather takes the candies out of the molds and he and his granddaughter enjoy them. How does the mass of the solid candy **compare** to the mass of the liquid in the mold?

    Ⓡ The mass of the solid candy is equal to the mass of the liquid in the mold.

    Ⓟ The mass of the solid candy is greater than the mass of the liquid in the mold.

    Ⓢ The mass of the liquid in the mold is greater than the mass of the solid candy.

    Ⓣ The mass of the liquid candy is less than the mass of the solid candy.

3 The gym teacher Mrs. Suez wants to order some basketballs for her students. Mrs. Suez orders the balls from a company in another state, so she has to pay shipping charges. The shipping charges are based on the weight of the package. Before she buys the basketballs, she must find the weight to make sure she can afford the balls and the cost of shipping. If Mrs. Suez wants to find **approximately** how much she will pay for shipping, what could she do?

    Ⓐ Ask the principal if she can have more money so she can afford the basketballs and the shipping.

    Ⓑ Call the company and tell them she won't buy the basketballs unless she doesn't have to pay for shipping.

    Ⓒ When the box arrives, put the box of basketballs on a scale and find out what the weight is.

    Ⓓ Multiply the weight of one basketball by the number of basketballs she wants to buy.

4 Martin is making a salad. He includes lettuce, tomatoes, onions, and carrots. Which statement correctly describes Martin's salad?

   Ⓕ Martin's salad is a compound.

   Ⓖ Martin's salad is a mixture.

   Ⓗ Martin's salad is a solution.

   Ⓘ Martin's salad is a formula.

5 What causes chemical weathering?

   Ⓐ sedimentary rock

   Ⓑ wind and plants

   Ⓒ acid rain

   Ⓓ decomposers

6 Carrie wants to see what exists in a drop of water. Which instrument should she use?

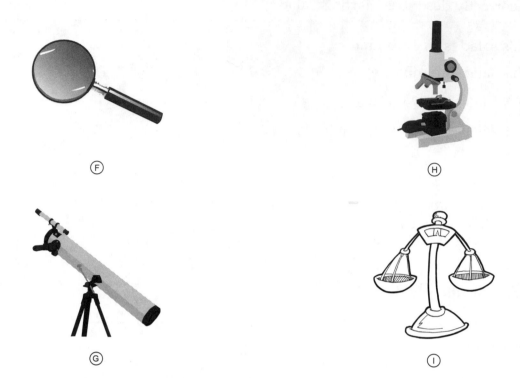

Ⓕ

Ⓗ

Ⓖ

Ⓘ

7 Look at this food chain.

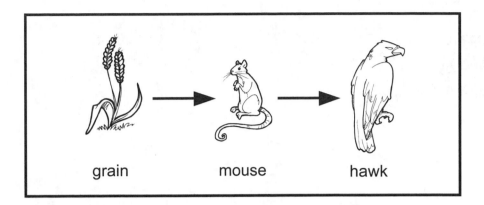

grain   mouse   hawk

Which organism is the producer and why? Which organisms are consumers and why?

_____

_____

_____

8 Kya's mom burns some logs in the fireplace. What forms of energy are released by the burning logs?

Ⓐ electric and solar

Ⓑ heat and light

Ⓒ heat and mechanical

Ⓓ electric and light

9 Mr. Reynaldo burns a candle in his classroom during science class. He asks his students to make observations about the burning candle.

Student	Observations
Kia	The burning candle gives off light.
Mark	The burning candle melts the wax.
Steve	The burning candle burns the wick.
Tara	The burning candle gives off electricity.

Which student's observation is incorrect?

Ⓕ Kia

Ⓖ Mark

Ⓗ Steve

Ⓘ Tara

10 Gabriel's mother makes some soup for lunch. Gabriel gets a bowl from the cupboard and her mom fills it with two large ladles of soup. As Gabriel carries the bowl to the kitchen table, the bowl begins to feel warm. Which of the following explains why the bowl became warm?

   Ⓐ   chemical change

   Ⓑ   energy transfer

   Ⓒ   physical change

   Ⓓ   loss of matter

11 In a certain ecosystem, the energy pyramid looks like the one below.

Sample Energy Pyramid for a Marine Ecosystem

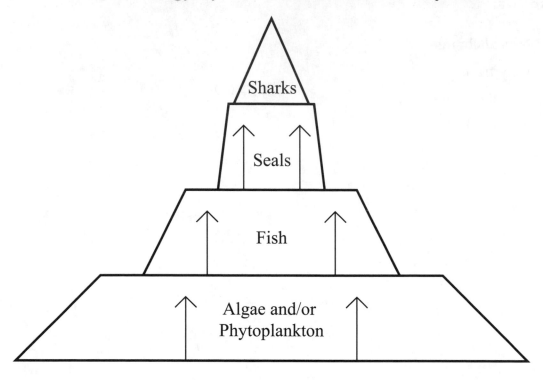

What would happen to the sharks if the fish population were destroyed by overfishing in the area?

Ⓕ The sharks would only eat seals because the fish they once ate are now gone.

Ⓖ The sharks' food supply would be less because the seals need the fish to survive.

Ⓗ The sharks' food supply would remain the same because the sharks only eat seals.

Ⓘ The sharks would eat algae because that level was not affected by the loss of fish.

12 Callie and Jorge are twins, and they weigh the same amount. On their birthday, they each received a black Mountain Bike XTZ. Callie is riding her bike on a flat path. Her brother Jorge is also riding his bike on a flat path, but he is pulling a cart behind his bike. There is nothing attached to Callie's bike. Callie and Jorge stop for a while, and then begin pedaling again. They want to be able to travel at the same speed and ride side by side. Which statement is **true**?

Ⓐ   Callie uses more force than Jorge uses to accelerate her bike.

Ⓑ   Jorge uses more force than Callie uses to accelerate his bike.

Ⓒ   Jorge uses less force than Callie uses to accelerate his bike.

Ⓓ   Callie and Jorge use the same amount of force to accelerate their bikes.

13 The dog barks while standing at point A.

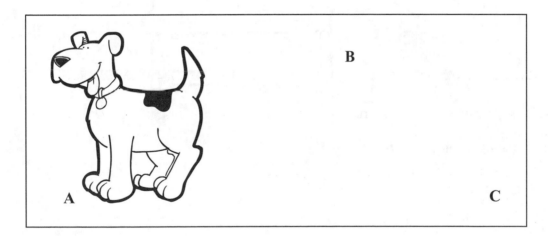

Why is the bark louder at point B than at point C?

Ⓕ   Sound waves are more condensed at point B.

Ⓖ   Sound waves cannot travel as far as point C.

Ⓗ   Sound waves are more condensed at point C.

Ⓘ   Sound waves only travel in one direction.

14 In science, work does not occur unless something is moved across a distance using force. Why would someone want to use a simple machine?

   Ⓐ Simple machines stop work.

   Ⓑ Simple machines eliminate work.

   Ⓒ Simple machines decrease work.

   Ⓓ Simple machines increase work.

15 Look at the picture of the boy and the piano.

What causes the piano to move?

   Ⓕ Force is applied by the boy.

   Ⓖ Gravity pushes the piano.

   Ⓗ The piano wheels pull the piano up.

   Ⓘ Inertia causes the piano to stay in motion.

16 Look at the picture below of a boy pushing a piano up a ramp.

Which of the following would reduce the effort required to push the piano up the ramp?

Ⓐ   the height of the ramp is decreased

Ⓑ   the height of the ramp is increased

Ⓒ   the weight of the piano is increased

Ⓓ   the weight of the ramp is reduced

17 Which statement is an example of erosion?

Ⓕ   Roots hold soil in place.

Ⓖ   Rain washes away a sand dune.

Ⓗ   A glacier deposits soil in a low-lying area.

Ⓘ   Decaying matter returns nutrients to the soil.

18 When Joaquin was in kindergarten, an oak tree grew on the other side of the creek. When Joaquin was in fifth grade, he saw that the oak tree was in the path of the creek's flow. What **most likely** caused this change?

Ⓐ The tree moved itself into the creek in order to get more water.

Ⓑ The flow of the creek changed its course.

Ⓒ Someone dug up the tree and replanted it in the creek.

Ⓓ A new oak tree grew out of the creek, and the original tree died.

19 What causes day and night?

READ
INQUIRE
EXPLAIN

_____

_____

_____

_____

_____

_____

20 When the Earth is between the Moon and the Sun, what is **true** about the Moon?

    Ⓕ The Moon is full because the entire lighted half can be seen.

    Ⓖ The Moon is new because the moon cannot reflect the Sun's light.

    Ⓗ The Moon is full because the Earth casts a shadow on the Moon.

    Ⓘ The Moon is partially lit because some of the Sun's light is reflected.

21 Why is the Sun central to life on Earth?

    Ⓐ The Sun is in between the Earth and the Moon.

    Ⓑ The Sun provides heat, light, and energy.

    Ⓒ The Sun warms the center of the Earth.

    Ⓓ The Sun keeps the Earth in orbit.

22 When compared to the Earth, which of the following describes the Moon?

    Ⓕ arid

    Ⓖ larger

    Ⓗ the same size

    Ⓘ more populated

23 Which of the following **best** describes the Sun?

(A) a constellation

(B) a galaxy

(C) a planet

(D) a star

24 Lu is working on his science project. Three topics in his science project are the brain, the spinal cord, and nerves.

System	One Function of System
Skeletal	supports muscles and organs
Nervous	interprets messages the body receives and respond to them
Digestive	helps our bodies to get energy from foods we ingest
Muscular	assists in body movement
Circulatory	moves blood through the body
Respiratory	transports gases to and from the circulatory system

What system of the human body is the subject of Lu's project?

(F) digestive

(G) nervous

(H) circulatory

(I) respiratory

Copying is Prohibited   © Englefield & Associates, Inc.

25 A diagram of two food chains is shown below.

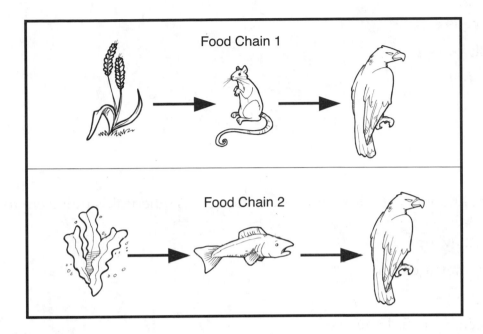

The arrows on each food chain point to what?

(A) the organism that is a predator

(B) the organism that releases energy

(C) the organism that is a carnivore

(D) the organism that takes in energy

26 Which statement is **not** true?

(F) Both plants and animals need water.

(G) Both plants and animals need shelter.

(H) Both plants and animals need food.

(I) Both plants and animals need a way to dispose of waste.

27 In human beings, what cells help form an outer layer that protects the human body?

    Ⓐ bone cells

    Ⓑ muscle cells

    Ⓒ nerve cells

    Ⓓ skin cells

28 Zebras are known for their stripes. When do zebras inherit this trait from their parents?

    Ⓕ when they are born

    Ⓖ before they are born

    Ⓗ when they die

    Ⓘ between birth and age one

29 Read this information about a food chain.

A fish eats a tadpole, and then an eagle eats the fish.

What is missing?

    Ⓐ what type of eagle ate the fish

    Ⓑ what ate the fish

    Ⓒ what the tadpole ate

    Ⓓ what time of day this happened

Go On

30 During the winter months, the temperature begins to drop in North America. During this time, bears hibernate. Why do bears hibernate?

(F) They need to sleep in order to hunt during the spring.

(G) Their bodies cannot handle the cold temperatures.

(H) They need to use the excess energy stored by their bodies.

(I) Their food supply is very small.

31 Why do plants have leaves?

(A) to capture energy from the Sun

(B) to change colors in the fall

(C) to capture oxygen

(D) to produce carbon dioxide

32 A rabbit depends on vegetation for food. Which describes a rabbit?

(F) first level predator

(G) first level producer

(H) first level consumer

(I) second level consumer

33 In an ecosystem, when an animal dies, its remains are broken down. What breaks down the animal's remains?

Ⓐ animals

Ⓑ consumers

Ⓒ decomposers

Ⓓ plants

34 Scientists look at tree rings to determine the age of a tree. For each year of a tree's life, it adds a layer (a ring) to its trunk and branches. Rings are thicker when resources are plentiful. Rings are thinner when resources are scarce. Which of the following will cause a tree to add a thick ring?

Ⓕ pollution

Ⓖ temperatures that are colder than normal

Ⓗ a large amount of rainfall

Ⓘ a drought

35 An eagle has sharp, curved talons. What does this characteristic **most likely** tell you about eagles?

Ⓐ Eagles use their talons to help them swim.

Ⓑ Eagles use their talons to transport their young.

Ⓒ Eagles use their talons to gather seeds.

Ⓓ Eagles use their talons to catch their prey.

36 In parts of the Northwestern United States, logging is destroying many forests. These forests are home to the spotted owl. Many people worry that logging will result in the extinction of the spotted owl. What is the **main** cause of extinction?

    Ⓕ fishing

    Ⓖ hunting

    Ⓗ global warming

    Ⓘ loss of habitat

37 A housing development has cut down half of the trees in a forest. What must the organisms that live in the forest do in order to survive?

    Ⓐ The organisms must compete with one another for the limited resources that are left in the habitat.

    Ⓑ The organisms must learn to get along with the people who will move into the houses.

    Ⓒ The organisms must stop having offspring in order to limit the strain on the resources.

    Ⓓ The organisms must migrate to another area that offers fewer resources.

38 Kylie's plant grows a little each week. Kylie created the chart shown below to show her results.

Day	Plant Height
Day 1	3 centimenters
Day 8	2 centimenters
Day 15	6 centimenters
Day 21	10 centimenters

What mistake did Kylie make?

F She stopped measuring the plant's height at Day 21.

G She should have measured the plant using inches.

H She did not measure the plant every day.

I She measured incorrectly on Day 8.

39 Four steps of the scientific method are listed below.

> **Steps of the Scientific Method**
>
> Step 1: State the Problem
> Step 2: Form a Hypothesis
> Step 3: Test the Hypothesis
> Step 4: Draw a Conclusion

During which step would a scientist analyze information from an experiment?

A Step 1

B Step 2

C Step 3

D Step 4

Use the information below and your knowledge of science to help you answer the question.

George wanted to determine whether a battery's cost affects how long it lasts. George bought four packs of batteries. All the batteries were the same size, but they were different brands. The brands George bought are listed from the least expensive to the most expensive: Brand A, Brand B, Brand C, and Brand D. George predicted that Brand D battery would last the longest. It was the most expensive.

George gathered together wires, a stopwatch, four of the same kind of light bulbs, and graph paper. George tested the four different brands of batteries by hooking up each of the batteries to a separate light bulb using wire. He then used his stopwatch to keep track of the length of time each bulb stayed lit. It took several days to gather his data.

After the experiment, George reviewed his results. The Brand D battery lasted the longest, 10 hours and 20 minutes. The Brand C battery came in second place; it lasted 9 hours and 17 minutes. Brand B was third; it lasted 7 hours and 30 minutes. Brand A only lasted for 5 hours and 58 minutes. George discovered that cost does relate to how long a battery lasts.

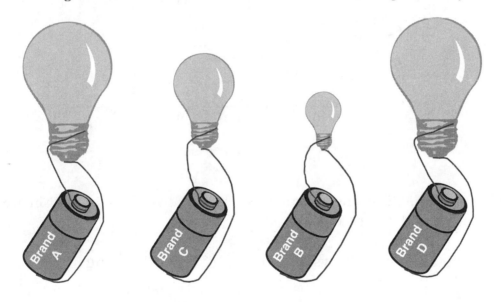

40 Based on what you know about George's experiment, what is **wrong** with the model above?

⒡ The light bulbs should all be different sizes.

⒢ The batteries should be different sizes.

⒣ The light bulbs should all be the same size.

⒤ The batteries should all be the same brand.

41 Niko looked up temperatures for his hometown in the almanac. He found the high temperature on January 1 for the years 1999–2003. He put this information in a graph.

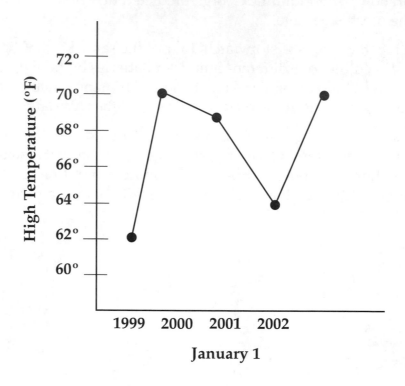

High Temperature for the First Day of the Year

Based on the temperatures he recorded in his graph, which is the **best** inference about the temperature on January 1, 2004?

Ⓐ The temperature will always be between 60° and 70° on January 1.

Ⓑ The temperature will always be below 70° on January 1.

Ⓒ The temperature will likely be between on 60° and 70° on January 1.

Ⓓ The temperature will likely be below 60° on January 1.

42 Chantell is measuring how long it takes for a container of water to boil. When the experiment finishes, Chantell stops the timing device. It reads 4:50. She learns that it took 4 minutes and 50 seconds for the container of water to boil.

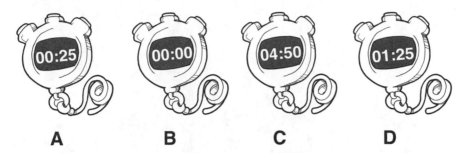

What did Chantell's stopwatch look like before the experiment began?

- Ⓕ Stopwatch A
- Ⓖ Stopwatch B
- Ⓗ Stopwatch C
- Ⓘ Stopwatch D

43 Which of the following is considered a testable hypothesis?

- Ⓐ Water slightly erodes loose topsoil.
- Ⓑ Seeds will grow without light.
- Ⓒ Trees grow in good soil.
- Ⓓ Animals will grow if they are happy.

This is the end of the Science Practice Tutorial.
Until time is called, go back and check your work or answer questions you did not complete. When you have finished, close your workbook.

Science Assessment

Directions for Taking the Science Assessment Test

In this Assessment you will answer 55 questions. For multiple-choice questions, you will be asked to pick the best answer out of four possible choices. Fill in the answer bubble to mark your selection. For a short-response or an extended-response question, write your answers on the lines that are given. Read each question carefully and answer it to the best of your ability. If you do not know an answer, you may skip the question and come back to it later. When you finish, check your answers.

Science Assessment

Use the information below and your knowledge of science to help you answer questions 1–4.

Dominick has several breakfast options. He can have a bowl of cereal with milk. He can have a piece of bread that has been toasted and is topped with butter. He can have a hard-boiled egg, or he can have a scrambled egg.

Dominick decides he would like to have a piece of toast and a bowl of cereal. He puts the bread in the toaster. While the bread is toasting, he fills his bowl with milk and cereal. The cereal is made of big wheat flakes. Dominick returns to the toaster. When the bread pops up, it is toasted. He puts his hand on the outside of the toaster; the outside of the toaster feels hot. Dominick cuts a pat from the stick of butter. When the butter hits the bread, it begins to melt.

1 What is **true** about Dominick's milk and cereal?

ⒶThe mixture of milk and cereal cannot be separated.

ⒷThe mixture includes two solids.

ⒸThe mixture includes a liquid and a solid.

ⒹThe mixture forms a new substance.

2 What type of change is Dominick's toast an example of, and why?

ⒻBread becoming toast is an example of a chemical change.

ⒼBread becoming toast is an example of a physical change.

ⒽToast becoming bread is an example of a physical change.

ⒾToast becoming bread is an example of a chemical change.

3 What is **most likely** true about the temperature of Dominick's toast?

Ⓐ The temperature of the toast was lower than the melting point of butter.

Ⓑ The temperature of the toast was at the melting point of butter or higher.

Ⓒ The temperature of the toast was at the boiling point of butter or higher.

Ⓓ The temperature of the toast was at the same temperature as the butter.

---

4 Write **one** reason why the outside of the toaster felt hot to Dominick.

READ
INQUIRE
EXPLAIN

_____

_____

_____

_____

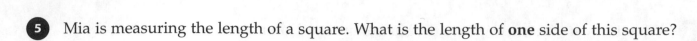
5 Mia is measuring the length of a square. What is the length of **one** side of this square?

  Ⓕ 1 centimeter

  Ⓖ 2 centimeters

  Ⓗ 1 inch

  Ⓘ 2 inches

6 In art class, Tenisha opens a jar of clay. She molds the clay into the shape of a horse.

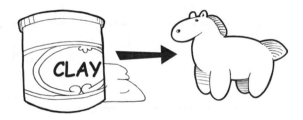

What type of change has taken place?

  Ⓐ an element change

  Ⓑ a compound change

  Ⓒ a physical change

  Ⓓ a chemical change

7 Where do producers get their energy from?

    Ⓕ herbivores

    Ⓖ carnivores

    Ⓗ consumers

    Ⓘ the Sun

8 In the experiment below, a light bulb is connected to a battery using wires. When all the connections are made between the battery and the bulb, the bulb lights. It takes energy to light the bulb.

Where does this energy come from?

    Ⓐ It is stored in the glass of the light bulb.

    Ⓑ It is stored in the battery.

    Ⓒ It is stored in the wire.

    Ⓓ It is stored in the metal base of the light bulb.

9   Charles' uncle likes to go camping. When he camps, he gathers small sticks to build a campfire. What purpose does this campfire serve?

Ⓕ   It helps Charles' uncle see at night and cook his dinner.

Ⓖ   It helps Charles' uncle see at night and catch his dinner.

Ⓗ   It helps Charles' uncle see during the day and keep warm at night.

Ⓘ   It helps Charles' uncle see during the day and sleep at night.

10   Tisha observes an ice cube that is melting. She then puts the ice cube into Cylinder A, which is filled with water. When she puts the ice cube in the water, it begins to melt more quickly than when it was not in the cylinder. Which statement explains why the ice cube melted more quickly in the water?

Ⓐ   The temperature of the water was cooler than the air temperature.

Ⓑ   The temperature of the air was the same as the water temperature.

Ⓒ   The temperature of the air was warmer than the water temperature.

Ⓓ   The temperature of the water was warmer than the air temperature.

11   Shawn is holding a stopwatch. What can Shawn measure with his stopwatch?

Ⓕ   the time it takes for a ball to travel across the floor

Ⓖ   the distance a ball travels across the floor

Ⓗ   the temperature of the air in the room

Ⓘ   the amount of light that enters the room

12 Maria wants to test how far she can throw a baseball. She throws the ball. It rises into the air and then begins to fall back down to the ground. What causes the ball to drop?

Ⓐ water vapor

Ⓑ gravity

Ⓒ wind

Ⓓ magnetism

13 Kyle's mom is rearranging the furniture in the living room. The items to be moved and their weights are given in the table below.

Sofa	90 lbs
Chair	35 lbs
Entertainment center	70 lbs
Bookshelf	20 lbs
Side table	15 lbs

Which piece of furniture requires the least amount of force to be moved?

Ⓕ side table

Ⓖ bookshelf

Ⓗ chair

Ⓘ sofa

14 How will a force in the same direction as motion affect speed?

READ
INQUIRE
EXPLAIN

_____

_____

_____

_____

15 Look at the picture below of a boy pushing a piano up a ramp.

If the boy stopped pushing the piano, what would happen to the piano?

(A) It would move down the ramp.

(B) It would continue to move up the ramp.

(C) It would remain in place on the ramp.

(D) It would move up the ramp at a slower pace.

16 During the water cycle, water that is stored on Earth turns from a liquid to a gas known as water vapor. The water vapor cools to form clouds. When the water vapor reaches a certain temperature, the water vapor turns back into a liquid and falls to the ground. What are the names of the stages in the water cycle?

Ⓕ evaporation, condensation, precipitation

Ⓖ vaporizing, condensation, rain

Ⓗ evaporation, conduction, precipitation

Ⓘ evaporation, concentration, rain

17 Which statement is **not** true about glaciers?

Ⓐ Glaciers can create cliffs by cutting into Earth.

Ⓑ Glaciers can create rivers by carving a path in the soil.

Ⓒ Glaciers can create valleys by removing soil.

Ⓓ Glaciers can create forests by removing soil.

18 A mountain stands close to the ocean. The mountain is east of the ocean, and the wind is moving from west to east. In general, when compared to the opposite side, the side of the mountain that is closest to the ocean receives how much rainfall?

Ⓕ less rainfall because most clouds move to the other side

Ⓖ more rainfall because of the effects of the water vapor coming off the ocean

Ⓗ the same amount of rainfall because the rate of precipitation is the same

Ⓘ no rainfall because clouds move to the other side

19 The contour map below shows several layers of the Earth.

The Contour Map of the Earth's Layers

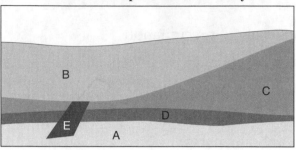

What **most likely** caused Layer E to form the way it did?

_____

_____

_____

_____

20 The contour map below shows several layers of the Earth.

The Contour Map of the Earth's Layers

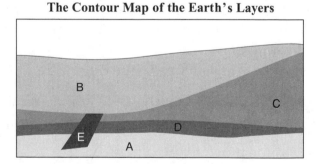

Which layer is the oldest?

Ⓐ Layer B

Ⓑ Layer D

Ⓒ Layer E

Ⓓ Layer A

21 When a hemisphere of the Earth is tilted away from the Sun, what occurs in that hemisphere?

    (F) fall

    (G) winter

    (H) spring

    (I) summer

22 How often does the Moon completely orbit the Earth?

    (A) about once a day

    (B) about once a week

    (C) about once a month

    (D) about once a year

23 What phase of the Moon is missing in the diagram?

Phases of the Moon

New Moon   **Full Moon**

 F

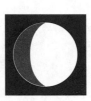

H

 G

I

24 Many scientists are working on ways to gather the Sun's energy and use it for heat, electricity, and power. Although using solar energy has a lot of potential, there are also problems. What is **one** problem with solar energy?

    Ⓐ The Sun's energy cannot be captured.

    Ⓑ The Sun's energy is not renewable.

    Ⓒ The Sun isn't always shining.

    Ⓓ The Sun is always shining.

25 Which statement is **true** about our solar system?

    Ⓕ Earth is the center of the solar system.

    Ⓖ The Sun is the center of the solar system.

    Ⓗ Mars is the center of the solar system.

    Ⓘ Mercury is the center of the solar system.

26 A beehive and a flowerbed are both present in Karl's back yard. If the beehive is destroyed, how will the flowers be affected?

    Ⓐ The flowers may have fewer resources.

    Ⓑ The flowers may grow larger because there is more room.

    Ⓒ The flowers may not be pollinated.

    Ⓓ The flowers may not have to compete for resources.

27 Which statement is **true**?

    ⓕ Consumers are a food source for producers.

    ⓖ Producers are a food source for consumers.

    ⓗ Producers are not a food source.

    ⓘ Consumers are not a food source.

28 What is **true** about the gas exhaled by animals and the gas taken in by plants?

    Ⓐ Animals exhale oxygen, and plants take in oxygen.

    Ⓑ Animals exhale carbon dioxide, and plants take in carbon dioxide.

    Ⓒ Animals exhale oxygen, and plants take in carbon dioxide.

    Ⓓ Animals exhale carbon dioxide, and plants take in oxygen.

29 Kara went to the pet store. She bought a parrot. When she brought the parrot home, she put it in a special birdcage. What behavior might the new parrot learn?

    ⓕ how to eat food

    ⓖ how to say a few words

    ⓗ how to drink water

    ⓘ how to build a nest

30 Which behavior represents an organism changing its environment to meet its needs?

Ⓐ   a bird building a nest

Ⓑ   a bird drinking from a puddle

Ⓒ   a bird eating berries on a bush

Ⓓ   a bird resting on a tree branch

31 What is **one** way that seasonal changes affect organisms?

Ⓕ   The supply of resources does not change.

Ⓖ   The supply of resources is always changing.

Ⓗ   The supply of resources is always restricted.

Ⓘ   The supply of resources is always increasing.

32 Which of the following improves the ability of birds to survive?

Ⓐ   They build their nests on the ground where they are easily seen.

Ⓑ   They limit the number of offspring they produce.

Ⓒ   They never leave their nests in order to protect their habitat.

Ⓓ   They migrate to warmer climates when necessary.

33 A food chain shows the flow of energy.

$$? \longrightarrow \text{plants} \longrightarrow \text{gazelle} \longrightarrow \text{lion}$$

What is missing from the food chain?

Ⓕ carbon monoxide

Ⓖ photosynthesis

Ⓗ the Sun

Ⓘ fertilizer

34 In a tundra ecosystem, the temperature rises above 32° F less than 60 days a year. In a deciduous forest ecosystem, the average temperature is 50° F. What can you conclude about the life cycle of a tundra plant?

Ⓐ It is more varied than a plant's life cycle in the deciduous forest.

Ⓑ It is equal to a plant's life cycle in the deciduous forest.

Ⓒ It is longer than a plant's life cycle in the deciduous forest.

Ⓓ It is shorter than a plant's life cycle in the deciduous forest.

35 Lions are predators. They feast on many different types of prey, such as giraffes, gazelles, and wildebeests. What characteristic must these predators have?

Ⓕ the ability to climb trees

Ⓖ the ability to hunt

Ⓗ the ability to use weapons

Ⓘ the ability to swim

36 During one experiment, Jane found that it takes 12 seconds for a pinwheel to stop spinning. Which statement is a valid conclusion?

    Ⓐ   Friction caused the pinwheel to spin.

    Ⓑ   All pinwheels will stop spinning after 12 seconds.

    Ⓒ   The pinwheel begins to spin when a force acts upon it.

    Ⓓ   All less expensive pinwheels will spin for less than 12 seconds.

37 Tara rolls a ball along the ground. Each time she rolls it, the ball goes farther than it did before. Which graph shows the results of Tara's experiment?

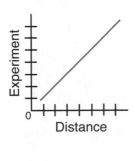

    Ⓕ

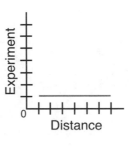

    Ⓗ

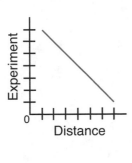

    Ⓖ

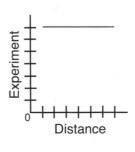

    Ⓘ

Go On ▶

38 Jean is in the fifth grade. Jean predicts that all the students in his fifth-grade class will be 68 inches tall by the age of 21. Jean must support his prediction at the fifth-grade science fair. What is **true** about Jean's prediction?

Ⓐ It cannot be tested.

Ⓑ It can never be proven true.

Ⓒ It can be supported with indirect evidence.

Ⓓ It can be proven true with statistics about the average height of human beings.

39 Mrs. Crator's class has an ant farm with 5 ants in their classroom. Each day, one student drops five pellets of food into the ant farm. Mrs. Crator wants to conduct an investigation to find out what would happen if the ant population in the ant farm doubled but the amount of pellets dropped into the farm stayed the same.

READ
INQUIRE
EXPLAIN

Design a procedure Mrs. Crator's class could follow to test what would happen if the ant population doubled but the amount of pellets dropped into the farm stayed the same.

_____

_____

_____

_____

_____

_____

_____

_____

_____

_____

_____

_____

40 Which statement is **true** about a compass?

Ⓕ A compass contains a magnet that has a north pole pointing to the magnetic north.

Ⓖ A compass contains a barometer that has a north pole pointing to the magnetic north.

Ⓗ A compass contains a battery that has a south pole pointing to the magnetic south.

Ⓘ A compass contains a thermometer that has a north pole pointing to the magnetic north.

41 What would happen to the fish in a river if pollution killed the plant life in the river?

Ⓐ The fish would have less competition for oxygen, so their populations would increase.

Ⓑ The fish would not have food to eat, so their populations would decrease.

Ⓒ The fish would not have enough light, so their populations would decrease.

Ⓓ The fish would have more space, so their population would increase.

42 What change happens to water when it is cooled to 0° C?

Ⓕ It forms a solution.

Ⓖ It starts to change from a liquid to a solid.

Ⓗ It starts to change from a gas to a liquid.

Ⓘ It forms a mixture.

43 Pelicans eat fish. For the pelican, fish is the **best** source of what?

    Ⓐ oxygen

    Ⓑ energy

    Ⓒ water

    Ⓓ vitamin C

44 What is a way that plants depend on animals?

    Ⓕ Certain animals produce the oxygen plants need.

    Ⓖ Certain animals produce energy for plants.

    Ⓗ Certain animals help some plants spread their seeds.

    Ⓘ Certain animals produce the water plants need.

45 Soil is made up of different parts, or ingredients. Which part of soil is made up of the decayed remains of plants and animals?

    Ⓐ clay

    Ⓑ sand

    Ⓒ silt

    Ⓓ humus

46 It is very important to keep the details correct when collecting what type of information during an experiment?

(F) results

(G) data

(H) estimates

(I) predictions

47 The drawing shows a model of the Sun, the Earth, and the Moon.

What is wrong with this model?

(A) The Earth should be smaller than the Sun and the Moon.

(B) The Sun should be larger than the Earth and the Moon.

(C) The Moon should be larger than the Earth.

(D) The Earth should be smaller than the Moon but larger than the Sun.

48 A group of Scouts go camping in the Rocky Mountains. The temperature drops quite low at night, so the group builds a campfire to sit around. The Scouts are happy to warm their hands and feet by the fire. What type of energy is helping to keep the Scouts warm?

(F) light energy

(G) sound energy

(H) motion energy

(I) heat energy

49 Plants, like all organisms, have certain basic needs to survive. Two basic needs are water and carbon dioxide. What is another basic need for a plant's survival?

(A) fertilizer

(B) soil

(C) sunlight

(D) roots

50 Which of the following describes an adaptation that allows a living thing to meet its need for food?

Ⓕ a fish's gills

Ⓖ a giraffe's neck

Ⓗ a plant's flowers

Ⓘ an insect's exoskeleton

51 The human body is composed of many systems, such as the digestive system and the nervous system. If your teacher discussed your skull, bones in your leg, your backbone, and your ribs, what system of the body would she be talking about?

Ⓐ skeletal system

Ⓑ circulatory system

Ⓒ respiratory system

Ⓓ immune system

52 The American pelican can be seen around the inland and coastal waters of Florida. Owls, macaws, sea gulls, and turkeys are other birds that can be found in Florida. Each of these birds have developed in a way that **best** suits their environment. Which bird can be found in the same ecosystem as pelicans?

Owl

(F)

Seagull

(H)

Macaw

(G)

Turkey

(I)

Go On

53 Water is found on Earth in its different states because of varying conditions.

READ
INQUIRE
EXPLAIN

Write **one** example of when water could be found as a solid.

_____

_____

_____

Write **one** example of when water could be found as a liquid.

_____

_____

_____

Write **one** example of when water could be found as a gas.

_____

_____

_____

Copying is Prohibited   © Englefield & Associates, Inc.

54 The living things below are connected in a food chain.

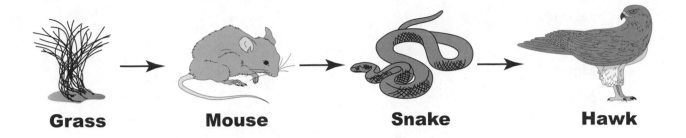

Grass   **Mouse**   **Snake**   **Hawk**

What would happen if the plants in the area died from pollution?

Ⓐ   The population of living things higher on the food chain would increase.

Ⓑ   The population of the living things higher on the food chain would decrease.

Ⓒ   The population of the living things higher on the food chain would stay the same.

Ⓓ   The population of only insects would decline.

55 The solar system is made up of many components. Which of the following is **not** a basic component of the solar system?

Ⓕ galaxies

Ⓖ Sun

Ⓗ Moon

Ⓘ planets

This is the end of the Science Assessment.
Until time is called, go back and check your work or answer questions you did not complete. When you have finished, close your workbook.

Notes

Notes

Notes

Notes

Show What You Know® on the 5th Grade FCAT Additional Products

Show What You Know® on the 5th Grade FCAT, Parent/Teacher Edition

Flash Cards for Reading, Mathematics, and Science

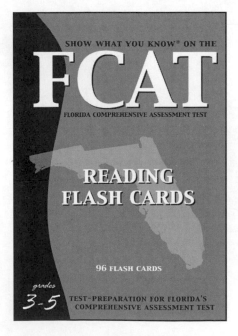
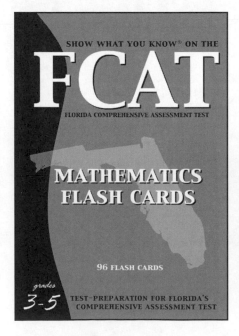
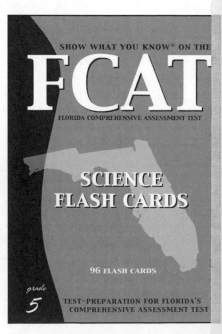

For more information, call our toll-free number: 1.877.PASSING (727.7464)
or visit our Web site: www.passthefcat.com